The Official EPAKS Guide to Long Form One

© 2014 EPAKS Publications

Pompano Beach, FL USA

All Rights Reserved

No part of this work may be reproduced in any form or by any means - graphic, electronic, or mechanical, including (but not limited to) photocopying, recording, taping, or information storage and retrieval systems - without the express written permission of the publisher.

Products that are referred to in this document may be either trademarks, registered trademarks, and / or copyrights of the respective owners. The publisher and the author make no claim to these trademarks and / or copyrights.

While every precaution has been taken in the preparation of this document, the publisher, author, and / or contributors assume no responsibility for errors or omissions, or for damages or injuries resulting from the use of information contained in this document or from the use of videos from which this document may refer. In no event shall the publisher and the author be liable for any loss of profit or any other commercial and / or personal damage caused or alleged to have been caused directly or indirectly by this document.

The reader should consult a qualified doctor's approval before attempting any physical activities presented in this document.

ISBN: 0-9769823-0-2

Publisher
  EPAKS Publishing
Author
  Ken Herman
Illustrations
  Ken Herman
  Ed Parker Jr.
  Marc Wolpert
Cover Design
  Marc Wolpert
  Ken Herman
Proof Readers
  Alexander Perez
  Steven Saviano
  Martin Seck
  Kit Herman
  Anthony Ramirez

Special thanks to:

those who contributed their time and efforts toward the development of this publication. Your efforts are appreciated and were invaluable to its development. You should be proud.

Also, no EPAKS publication would be complete without a special thank you to the person who made this all possible - Senior Grand Master and founder of the American Kenpo system - Edmund Kealoha Paker Senior: You are greatly missed.

In loving memory of our founder
SGM Edmund Kealoha Parker Senior
3/19/1931 - 12/15/1990

Table of Contents

Part I	Introduction	9
Part II	History of Long Form One	11
	2.1 During SGM Parker's Life	14
	2.2 After SGM Parker's Death	16
Part III	The Salutation and "Signifying"	18
	3.1 The Salutation	19
	Salutation Standard Exection	21
	Salutation Standard Execution - Illustration	26
	Salutation Variations	43
	3.2 "Signifying" a Form	44
	"Signifying" with Salutation - Illustration	46
	"Signifying" Variations	63
Part IV	Execution of Long Form One	65
	4.1 Non-Permanent Variations	67
	4.2 Non-Destructive Variations	68
	4.3 Various "Standards"	70
	4.4 Form Standard Execution	72
	4.5 Form Standard Execution - Illustration	90
	4.6 Form Standard Execution - Video	153
Part V	Understanding American Kenpo Forms	154
	5.1 Understanding Long Form One	157
	The Design of Long Form One	159

© 2014 EPAKS Publications

	Why Long Form One?	161
	Long Form One vs Short Form One	163

Part VI   Basics of Long Form One   165

6.1 Quick Reference of Basics	167
6.2 Basics Utilized in Long Form One	169

Part VII   Analysis of Long Form One   176

7.1 Intra vs Inter Form Analysis	179
7.2 Beginning / Intermediate Analysis	181
Walk-Through Analysis	183
Summary	191
7.3 Advanced Analysis	197
Walk-Through Analysis	199
Summary	205
7.4 Reverse / Opposite	208
Blocks	209
Strikes	214
Foot Maneuvers	218
Body Maneuvers	220
Torque Analysis Only - Triple Block Section Only	221
7.5 Principles / Rules / Theories / Concepts / Definitions	230

Part VIII   Improving Your Execution of Long Form One   234

8.1 General Errors	236
Timing	237
Gaze	238
Breathing	239
8.2 Stances	241
Stance Errors	244
Meditating Horse	245
Neutral Bow	247
Forward Bow	250

© 2014 EPAKS Publications

45 degree Cat	253
Reverse Bow	255
Fighting Horse	258

8.3 Foot Maneuvers — 260

Foot Maneuver Errors	**262**
Step Out to Meditating Horse	263
Step Through	264
Cover	266

8.4 Blocks — 268

Block Errors	**269**
Inward Block	270
Vertical Outward Block	271
Upward Block	273
Downward Block	275
Inside Downward - Palm Up	277
Inside Downward - Palm Down	278
Push-Down	279

8.5 Strikes — 282

Strike Errors	**283**
Straight Punch (including Isolation)	284
Outward Elbow	288
Isolation - Angled Punches	290
Isolation - Uppercut Punch	292

8.6 Improvement Priorities — 294

Part IX Frequently Asked Questions — 296

9.1 What is the timing of Long Form One?	297
9.2 Why is Long Form One NOT a 'defense only' form?	298
9.3 Why is the first offensive move in Long Form One the straight punch?	299
9.4 If American Kenpo is a strong sided system, why is the first punch a left?	301

© 2014 EPAKS Publications

9.5 What is the Primary Power Principle of the Straight Punch in Long Form One	302
9.6 Does the back foot settle with the block or the punch?	303
9.7 Why is there only one cat stance near the beginning of the form?	304
9.8 Why are there triple blocks in the second half of Long Form One?	306
9.9 Why do we step forward on the first downward block?	307
9.10 Why is there no forward bow when executing the triple blocks?	308
9.11 What are 'isolations' and why are they important?	309
9.12 What part of our fist do we punch with in Long Form One?	310
9.13 What type of Elbow is Executed in Long Form One?	311
9.14 How does Long Form One relate to Short Form One?	312
9.15 What is the difference between Thrusting and Hammering Methods of Execution?	313
9.16 What is the difference between an opposite and a reverse?	314
9.17 Why shouldn't we visualize an opponent while executing this form?	315
9.18 If this form is for someone just starting, a beginner, why does it have so much information?	316
9.19 If I'm not visualizing an imaginary opponent, where and what should I look at when doing the form?	317

© 2014 EPAKS Publications

Contents

9.20 How does leaning affect me?	318
9.21 Why is the form done in the "+" instead of another pattern?	319
9.22 Did SGM Parker create Long Form One?	320
9.23 What is meant by a 'dictionary' form?	321

Part X Quizzes 322

10.1 Multiple Choice - Beginner / Intermediate	323
10.2 Fill in the Blank - Beginner / Intermediate	330
10.3 Multiple Choice - Advanced	333
10.4 Fill in the Blank - Advanced	340

Part XI Quiz Answers 343

11.1 Multiple Choice Answers - Beginner / Intermediate	344
11.2 Fill in the Blank Answers - Beginner / Intermediate	345
11.3 Multiple Choice Answers - Advanced	346
11.4 Fill in the Blank Answers - Advanced	347

Part XII The Kenpo Kards 348

12.1 The Front of the Kard	350
12.2 The Back of the Kard	352

Part XIII Reverse and Opposite 355

© 2014 EPAKS Publications

Part XIV Categories and Catetory Completion 358

14.1 Category Completion - Example 360
14.2 Category Legend 361
14.3 Inter-Form Categories 362
14.4 Intra-Form Categories 364

Chapter 1 - Introduction

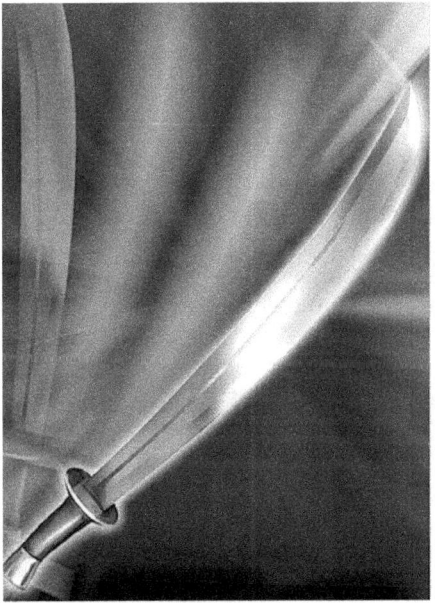

Long form one holds a very special place in the American Kenpo system. Why, one might ask? It isn't a very pretty form. Nor is it a very complex form. Its not even a very famous form, like say, Long Form Four. So what makes Long Form One so special? A number of factors. First, it's the first form in the system that SGM Parker actually created from scratch. Second. it is the first long form of the system. And as such, it lays out a number of guidelines to which all the other long forms of the system adhere. And thirdly, since it was created in the very early stages of American Kenpo's formulation, it can be used as a tool to help peer into the analytical mind of SGM Parker near the beginning of his illustrious career.

This book will explore all of these aspects of Long Form One, and more. It's goal is to not only help the reader get a complete understanding of Long Form One and its place in the American Kenpo system, but also to aid in understanding the analytical mind of SGM Parker.

Long Form One, as we practice it today, is not executed exactly as it was at the form's inception. SGM Parker incorporated small changes and enhancements to the form over time, but these changes stopped by the end of the 1960's. Although SGM Parker tried not make permanent changes to any of the forms that were already released to the general student population - in the early years, this was not always possible. This is because SGM Parker was teaching at the same time he was developing American Kenpo. As such, it is possible to still find some of his elder students (and their students) who have legitimate differences of execution from what is now considered the standard of execution. This book will not attempt to invalidate those differences, but instead not include them in the analysis of the form. What will be included is the final revision of the form as SGM Parker left it at the time of his death.

Chapter 2 - History of Long Form One

Although the general history of Long Form One is fairly well known, a precise history of one important date is not known - the exact creation date of the form. What is known, though, is that it was created by SGM Parker very early in the developmental stages of American Kenpo (in the mid to late 1950's). It is conjectured and probably true that SGM Parker got ample input and feedback from a number of sources during the form's development. Also, SGM Parker incorporated small changes and enhancements to the form over time, but all enhancements stopped by the mid 1960's.

Long Form One was created to be a direct follow up to Short Form One. All formal documentation from SGM Parker shows, and the majority of instructors teach, Long Form One as the second form of the American Kenpo system. Although there are a few instructors that teach Short Form Two as the second form. This situation came about because at first Long Form One was taught to beginners shortly after learning Short Form One. But, for a short period of time in the 1960's Long Form One was taught after Short Form Two - at Blue belt. Long Form One was soon placed back prior to Short Form Two - at Orange belt, where it stayed.

The logic for moving Long Form One after Short Form Two mostly surrounded the motivation to keep the shorter forms together while saving the longer forms for the slightly more advanced student. There is sound reasoning to this argument, and as such, of few of the instructors from that period opted to keep the order Short Form One, Short Form Two, Long Form One, Long Form Two even after the final shuffling.

The logic for keeping the original order of Short Form One, Long Form One, Short Form Two, Long Form Two deals with timing, logical sequencing of basics, and general flow through the forms. The timing argument says that the one-in-one timing forms should be kept together and the two-in-one timing forms should be kept together. The logical sequencing of basics argument says that Short Form One starts with defense only, front hand only, and retreating only. And, Long Form One starts with that foundation and then builds upon it - where as Short Form Two and Long Form Two continue to build up the foundation of Short Form One and Long Form One in complexity. The general flow argument says that the forms should flow numerically as follows: Short Form One, Long Form One, Short Form Two, Long Form Two, Short Form Three, Long Form Three, Form Four, etc. And, placing Short Form Two prior to Long Form One breaks the numerical flow.

History of Long Form One

One must also keep in mind that during all this period of flux there was no Yellow belt in the system, the self-defense techniques numbered thirty two per belt, and there were no extensions. Also, during part of this time, there were no self-defense techniques above '*The Back Breaker*' - i.e. Brown / Black belt self-defense techniques. So, the system was in flux in more ways than just deciding where to place Long Form One in the system.

Most people consider the American Kenpo System finalized at the point when SGM Parker published the '*Infinite Insight*' series. But, there were still a few changes in the works after the publication of that series, but these additions were never formally published and generally just being formalized and taught through small pockets of instructors - just as was done at the beginning of the formulation of the system. Given time these additions would have been stabilized and generally published to all. These changes included new forms, new books, and further study into weapons (namely the stick and the knife). If SGM Parker were still alive today, and with today's technology, one could count on the American Kenpo System being further enhanced and expanded than what existed at his death in 1990.

© 2014 EPAKS Publications

During SGM Parker's Life

The IKKA Accumulative Journal Version 1.0

(Copyright 1972)
This was the first published explanation of Long Form One. This description was considered the standard until the publication of the Infinite Insight series.

History of Long Form One 15

The Infinite Insights into Kenpo - book #5

(Copyright 1987)
This was the second, and most comprehensive, explanation of Long Form One. It's description gave not only the physical and pictorial narration of this form, but the first written comprehensive analysis of this form. This explanation is still considered by most to be the most widely read version of this form.

After SGM Parker's Death

The Encyclopedia of Kenpo

Version 1.0
(Copyright 1992)
This is the third published reference to Long Form One. The reference merely stated when the form should be taught at Orange belt.

The IKKA Accumulative Journal

Version 2.0
(Copyright 1992)
This is the last, official written reference to Long Form One that can be somewhat attributed to SGM Parker's direct influence.
It is an accumulation of revisions he was working on at the time of his death. It was compiled by his son Ed Parker Jr.

Chapter 3 - The Salutation and "Signifying"

In formal situations, the salutation and "signifying" are appended to the execution of a form. This practice adds clarity and formality to the form by allowing the viewer to not only determine the martial art style of the practitioner, but also the form which is intended to be performed; and whether the form will be modified from its standard execution.

The salutation is always appended to both the beginning and the end of the form. But, the signification gesture is only added to the beginning of the form.

© 2014 EPAKS Publications

The Salutation

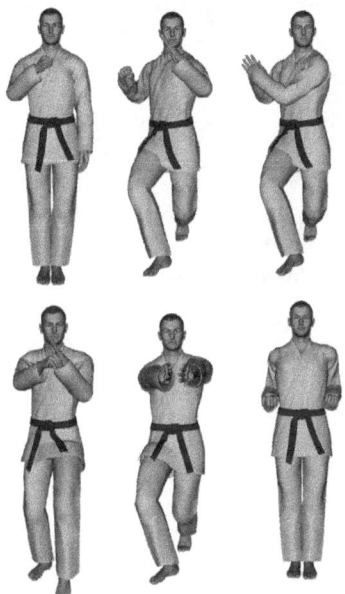

Original salutation

The original Kenpo salutation dates back to the boxer rebellion in China. At that time, the salutation was used as a gesture to show that you where one of the individuals fighting to bring back the Ming dynasty. The left hand over right fist represented the sun and the moon, which in Chinese characters formed the symbol of the Ming dynasty.

However, the salutation as executed today by American Kenpo practitioners is longer than the original and now only represents a linkage to its past heritage of Kenpo. The reason the modern day salutation is longer than the original is that SGM Parker added a "new" series of maneuvers to the end of the original salutation. This change was to represent a merging of the modern martial arts with those of the past.

'new' addition to salutation

Salutation Standard Exection

Note:
   H = Horizontal - Example: 6:00H
   V = Vertical - Example 12:00V

Note:
   Throughout the salutation, the foot and hand maneuver timing should be synchronized such that both start and come to a complete stop simultaneously.

---

1)   From an attention stance (toward 12:00H), bow and raise your head.
Meaning:
   Show respect to the art of kenpo.

---

2)   Step sideways, with your left foot (toward 9:00H), into a meditating horse stance (toward 12:00H) while simultaneously placing your left hand folded over (on a 1:30V - 7:30V line) your right fist (on a 10:30V - 4:30V line) parallel to your body in front of you, at chin level.
Meaning:
   Foot Maneuvers:
      I cast off the weak.
   Hand Maneuvers:
      I hide my treasure

---

3)   Bow your head into meditation.
Meaning:
   The meditation may vary depending upon the purpose of the salutation:
   Opening a Form:
      The practitioner is to clear the mind of any external thoughts.

© 2014 EPAKS Publications

Closing a Form:
> The practitioner is to meditate on the execution performance of the form.

---

4) Lift your head from meditation.
Meaning:
> You have finished meditation.

---

5) Raise both of your hands above your head (toward 12:00V), palms up (toward 12:00V), and without any loss of momentum draw your left foot (toward 3:00H) to your right foot while simultaneously lowering both of your hands in outward arches (left toward 9:00H - right toward 3:00H), ending into an attention stance (toward 12:00H).
Meaning:
> I draw the weak back to the strong.

Note:
> This is the point at which one would signify the form being performed.

---

6) Step forward, with your right foot (toward 12:00H) into a right front twist stance (toward 12:00H), while simultaneously bringing both your right clenched fist and left open hand over your right shoulder with your right fist facing forward (toward 12:00H) and your left palm facing over your right shoulder (toward 6:00H) covering your right fist.
Meaning:
> The scholar and the warrior meet...

The Salutation and "Signifying"

7) Step forward, with your left foot (toward 12:00H) into a left 45 degree cat stance (toward 12:00H) while simultaneously pushing both hands (maintaining contact with each other) forward (toward 12:00H) so your left open hand, palm facing downward and to your right (toward 1:30H), covers your left side of fist, knuckles facing forward (toward 10:30H) in front of you, at chin level.
Meaning:
and go forth into battle,...

---

8) Rotate and open both of your hands (maintaining contact with each other), in opposite directions, so that both palms face away from each other (left toward 9:00H - right toward 3:00H).
Meaning:
back to back they will work together...

---

9) Step back (left rear cross-over) with your left foot (toward 6:00H) into a right front twist stance (toward 12:00H) while simultaneously rotating both hands (still maintaining contact with each other) toward yourself, ending in a palm up position (toward 12:00V) in front of you at chin level. Draw your right foot back to your left foot (toward 6:00H) until both feet are side-by-side, while drawing and closing both hands simultaneously to chambered positions, palm up (toward 12:00V) at your sides, into a modified attention stance (toward 12:00H).
Meaning:
to bring the country back to the people.

Note:
Every move beyond this point was added by SGM Parker and is considered the "new" part of the salutation.

© 2014 EPAKS Publications

10) Step to your left with your left foot (toward 9:00H) into a horse stance while simultaneously raising both of your hands upward and in front of you (toward 12:00V) in slight outward arches, ending head high with palms away from you (toward 12:00H), while the thumbs and forefingers of both hands touch, forming a triangle [with the base of the triangle parallel to both the ground and your body (on a 9:00H - 3:00H line) and the tip of the triangle pointing straight upward (toward 12:00V)].
Meaning:
   I have no weapons.

11) Lower both hands (toward 6:00V) so your left hand folds over (on a 1:30V - 7:30V line) and covers your right fist (on a 10:30V - 4:30V line) parallel to your body in front of you at chin level.
Meaning:
   I hide my kenpo treasure

12) Continue the drop of your hands (toward 6:00V), to solar plexus level, while opening both of your hands simultaneously so the palms face each other (left toward 3:00H - right toward 9:00H) touching with the fingers pointing straight upward (toward 12:00V), as if praying.
Meaning:
   I pray for forgiveness for having to use my karate.

13) Raise both of your hands above your head (toward 12:00V), palms up (toward 12:00V) and without any loss of momentum draw your left foot (toward 3:00H) to your right foot while simultaneously lowering both of your hands in outward arches (left toward 9:00H - right toward 3:00H), ending into an attention stance (toward 12:00H).
Meaning:
   Close of the salutation

The Salutation and "Signifying"

14) Bow and raise your head.
Meaning:
　　Show respect to the art of kenpo.

Salutation Standard Execution - Illustration

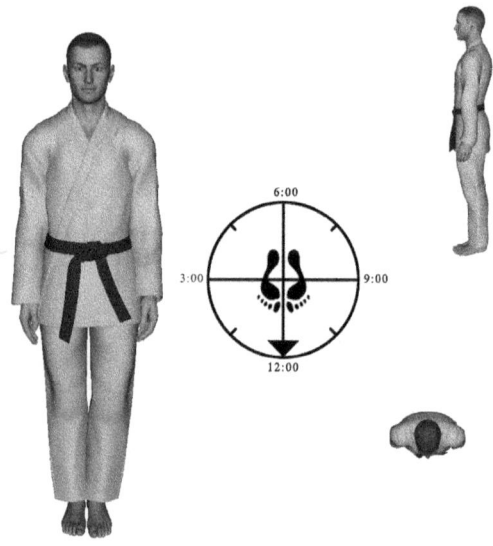

1) Opening Attention Stance

The Salutation and "Signifying"

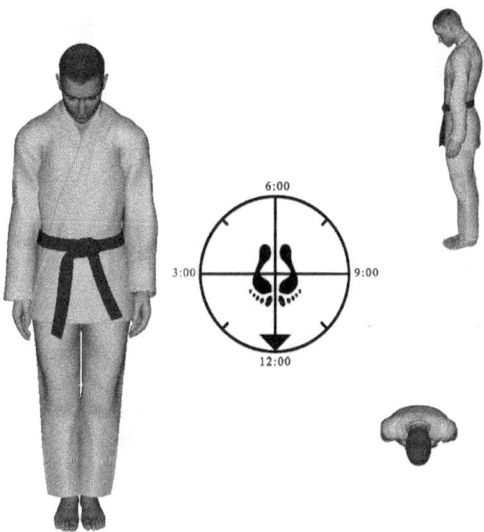

1b) Bow your head

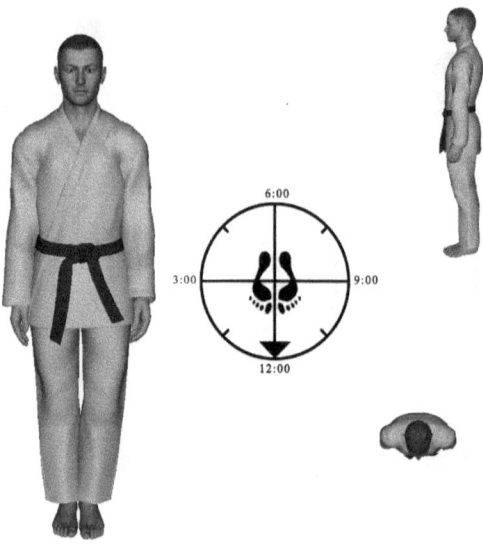

1c) Back to Attention Stance

The Salutation and "Signifying" | 29

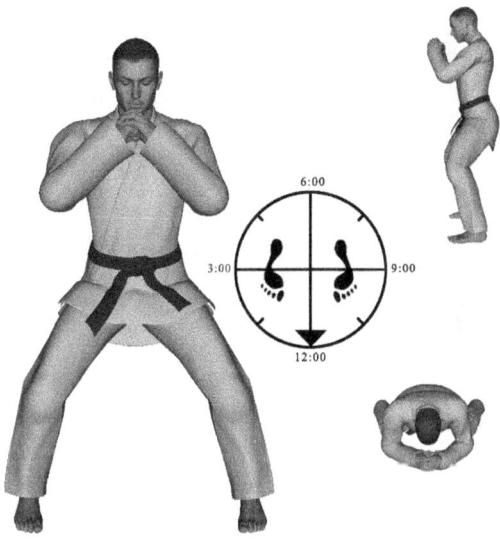

2, 3 & 4) Meditating Horse

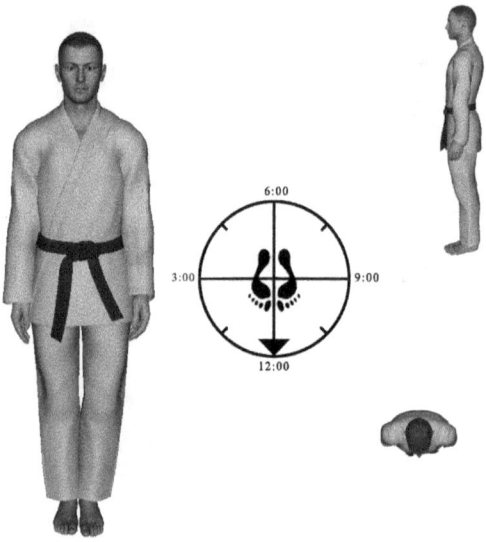

5) Back to Attention Stance

The Salutation and "Signifying"

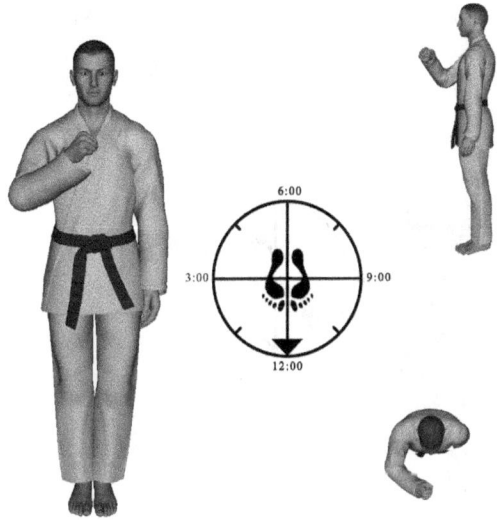

6a) the warrior

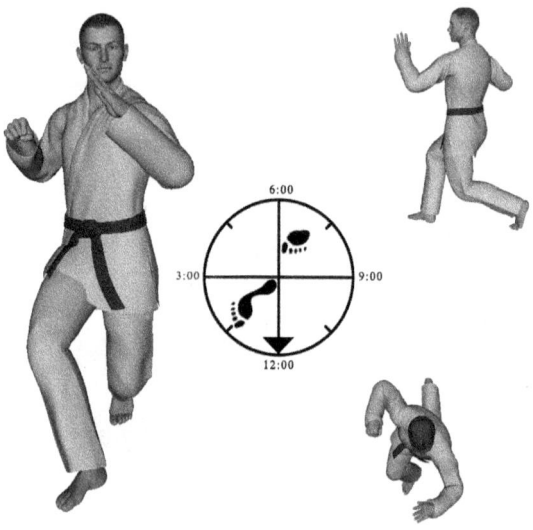

6b) and the scholar

The Salutation and "Signifying" | 33

6c) meet

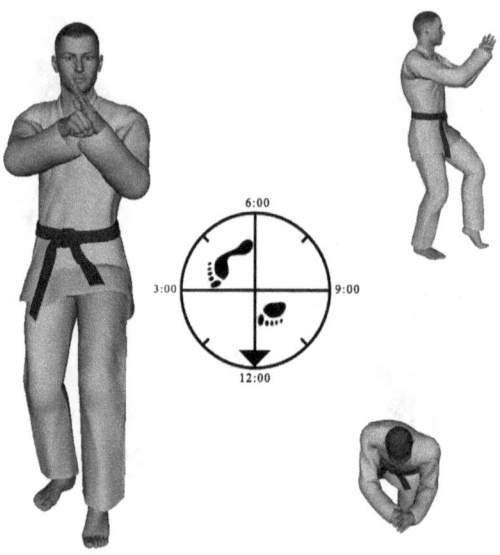

7) and go forth into battle

The Salutation and "Signifying" 35

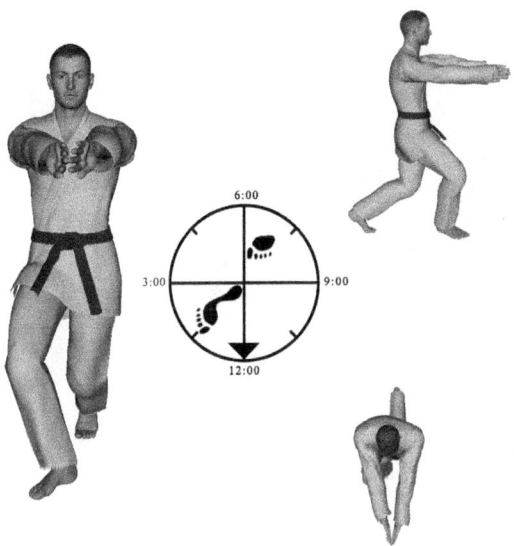

8) back to back they work

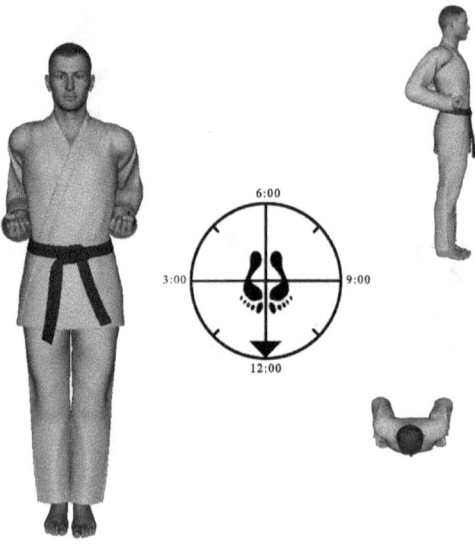

9) to bring the country back to the people

The Salutation and "Signifying"

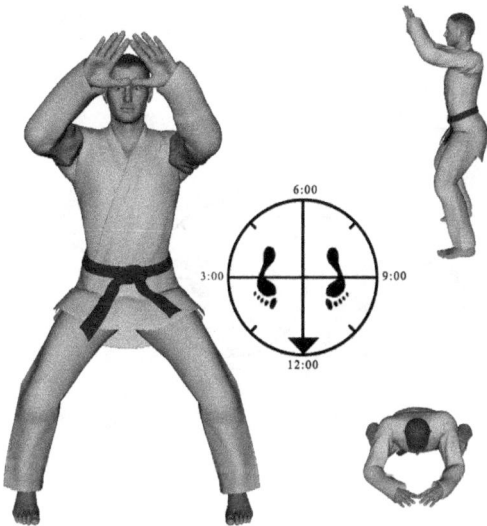

10) I have no weapons

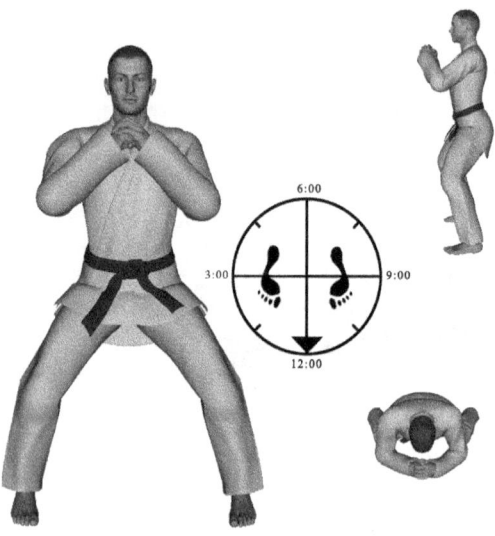

11) I hide my kenpo treasure

The Salutation and "Signifying" 39

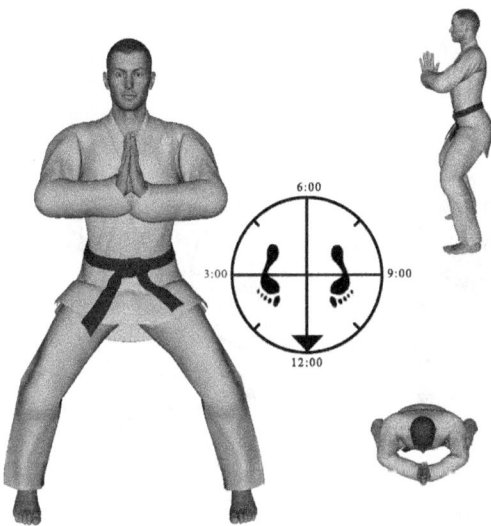

12) I pray for forgiveness
(for having to use my martial art)

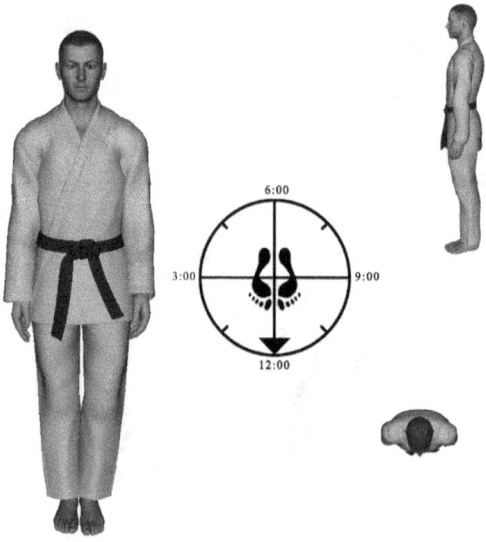

13) Back to Attention

The Salutation and "Signifying"

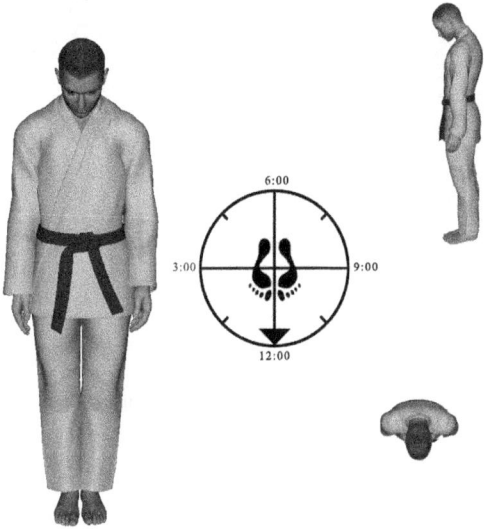

13a) Bow your head

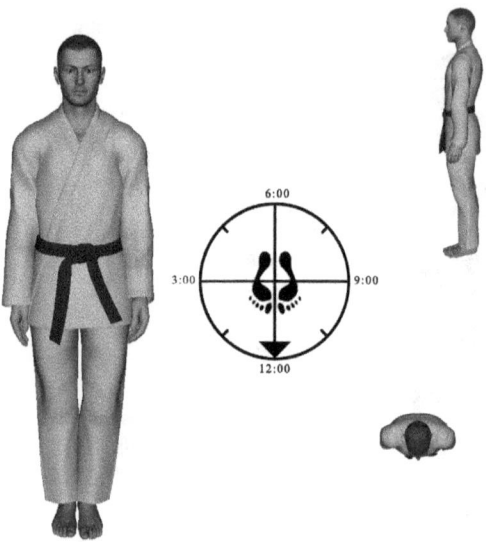

13b) Back to Attention

The Salutation and "Signifying"

Salutation Variations

The first four forms (Short Form One, Long Form One, Short Form Two, Long Form Two) each start from a horse stance. Therefore, the salutation for each of these forms is generally executed up to the last meditating horse stance, without drawing back to the final attention stance. The form is then executed from that point in the salutation. But, if the practitioner draws back to the final attention stance, thus finishing the full salutation - they may simply step back into a horse stance, and continue the execution of the form from that point.

One other common variation is the period of time meditation is performed during the salutation. This length of time can be skipped or can last for as long as a few seconds - but generally not longer, unless needed. This meditation is provided for the practitioner, in order for them to become calm and focused in both body and mind. So meditation length will vary by individual.

"Signifying" a Form

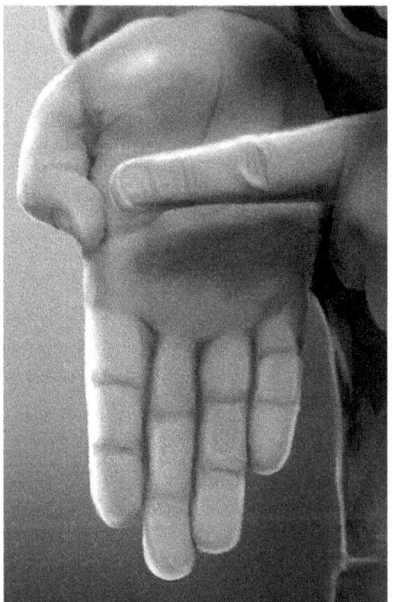

"Signifying" Long Form One

Signifying (or signing) is a hand gesture that is displayed prior to executing a form. In the case of Long Form One, the sign is a single finger (the index finger) extended and lay on top of the other opened hand (the backstop hand). This hand maneuver is typically done from an attention stance; displayed at waist level, facing front (i.e. perpendicular to the ground); and executed prior to the salutation. The backstop hand is positioned palm forward and fingers pointing to the ground. The signifying hand is placed perpendicular across the backstop hand, finger(s) pointing to the side, and palm facing the backstop hand.

The Salutation and "Signifying"   45

The history of signifying a form comes from the early competition days (prior to the 1970's). At this time, the participant was not allowed to talk to the presiding judges. So, to inform the audience and judges as to which form was to be executed, the signification was added at the beginning. Also, the display was shown on both sides of the body, so as to cover a 180 degree radius.

"Signifying" with Salutation - Illustration

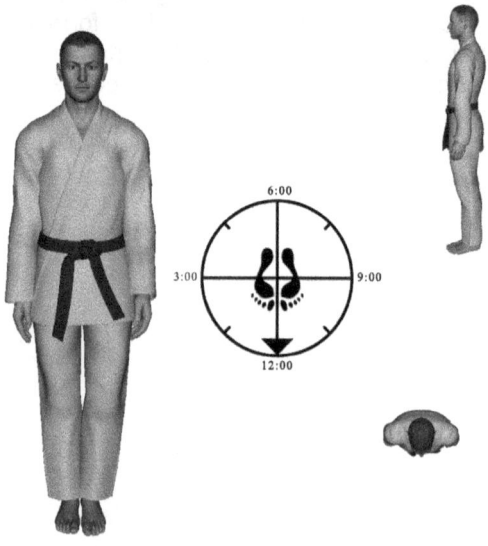

1) Opening Attention Stance

The Salutation and "Signifying" — 47

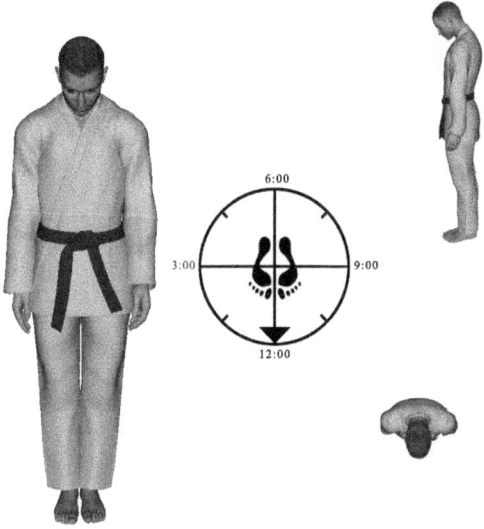

1b) Bow your head

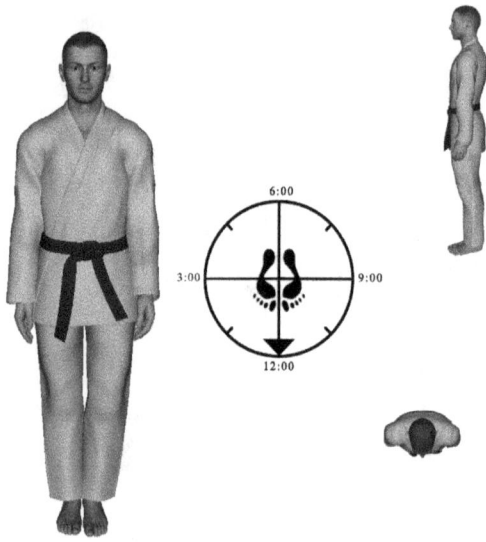

1c) Back to Attention Stance

The Salutation and "Signifying" | 49

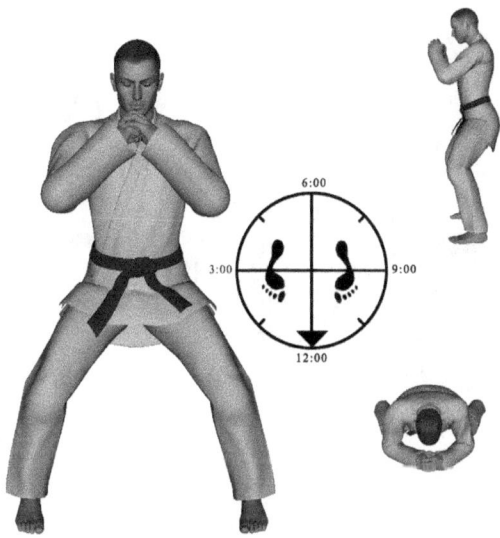

2, 3 & 4) Meditating Horse

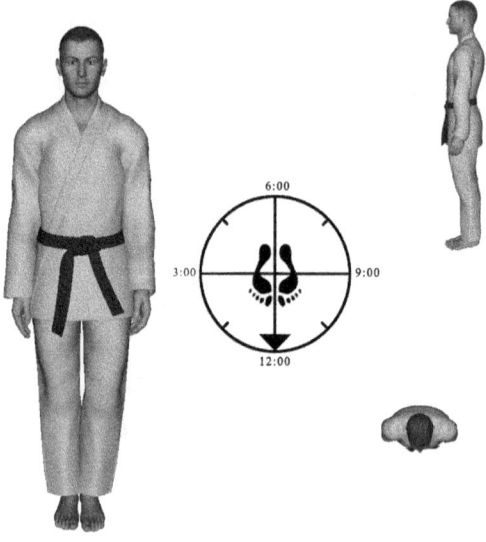

5) Back to Attention Stance

The Salutation and "Signifying" — 51

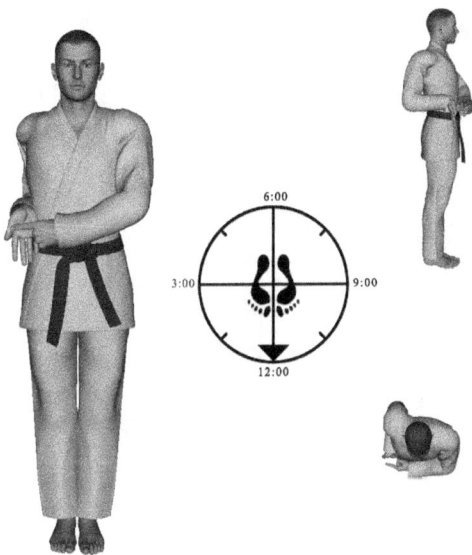

6) Signify on right side

52 The Official EPAKS Guide to Long Form One

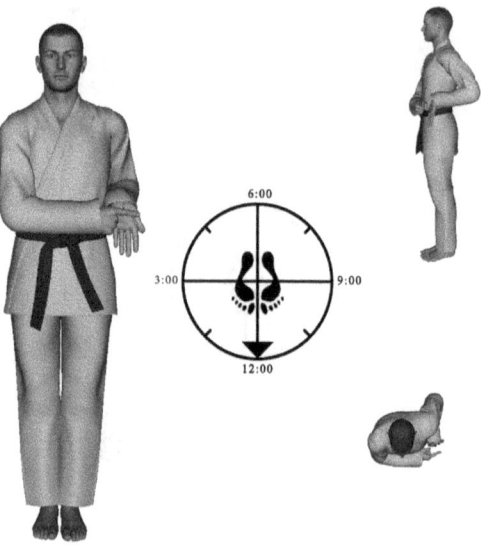

7) Signify on left side

The Salutation and "Signifying"

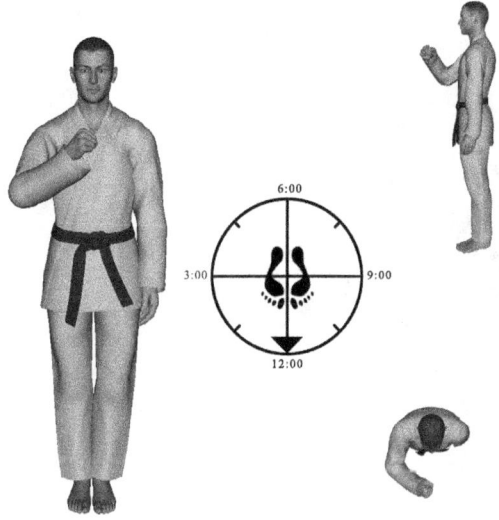

8a) the warrior

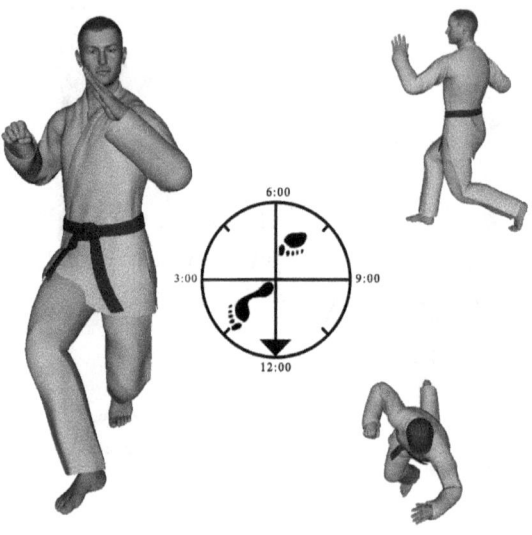

8b) and the scholar

The Salutation and "Signifying"

8c) meet

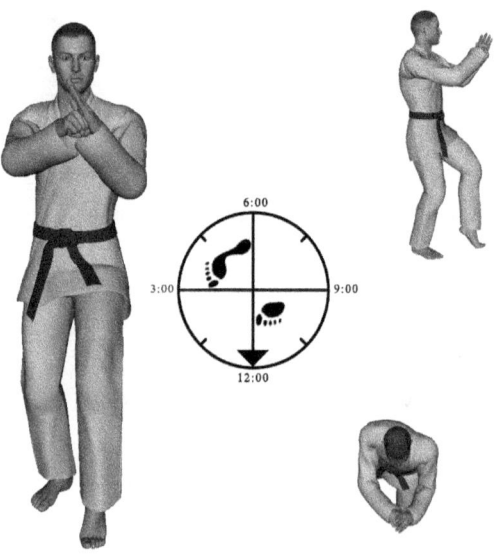

9) and go forth into battle

The Salutation and "Signifying" 57

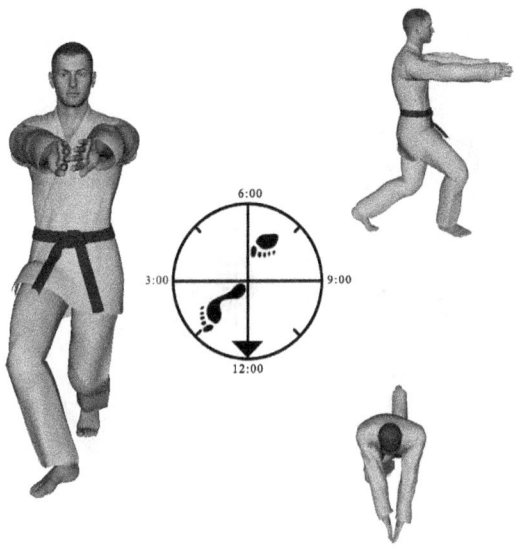

10) back to back they work

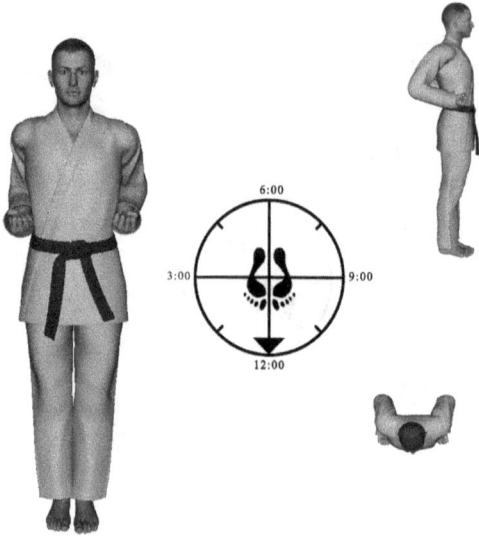

11) to bring the country back to the people

The Salutation and "Signifying"

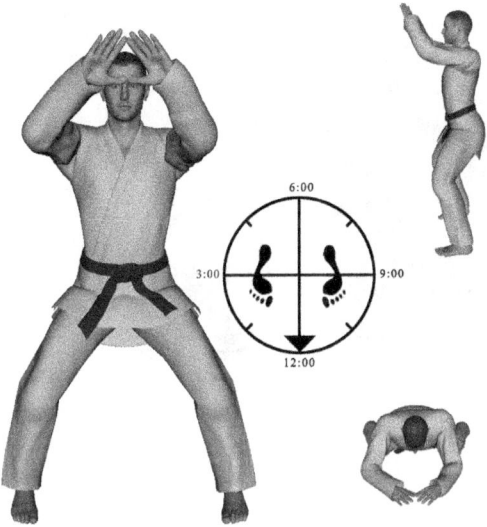

12) I have no weapons

13) I hide my kenpo treasure

The Salutation and "Signifying" 61

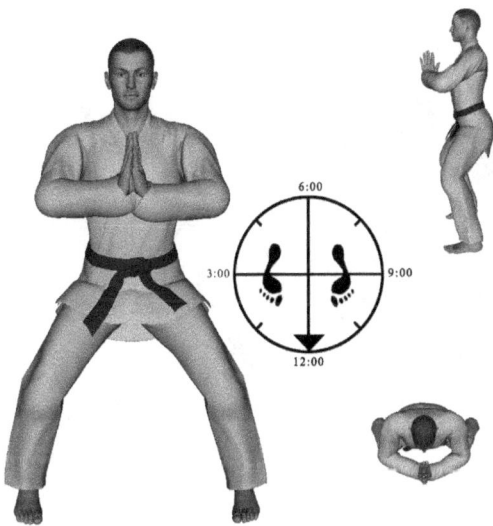

14) I pray for forgiveness
(for having to use my martial art)

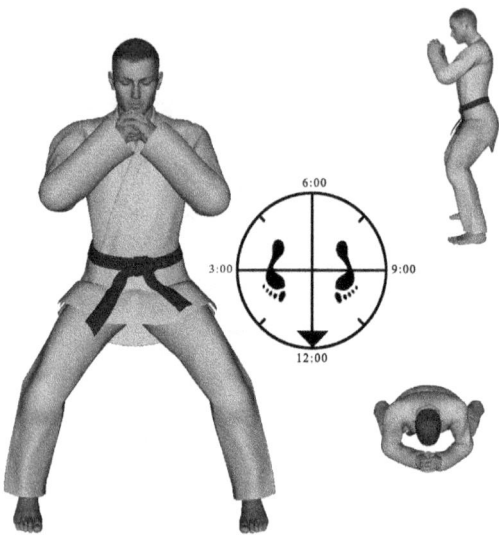

15) Back to Meditating Horse

"Signifying" Variations

There are a number of variations to signifying that have appeared over time which have become part of the standard way of signifying a form. Some of the variations are widely used, some are not well known, but each of the variations is optionally applied as needed.

The first variation is whether the form is signified at all. At first, only the upper forms (short three and above) were signified and utilized the salutation. But over time, signifying and the salutation were considered appropriate for all forms (but typically not sets). An added benefit to adding the signification and salutation to the lower forms was that it made the forms a great deal longer and gave the form a greater feeling of complexity. If compared to Short Form One, the signification and salutation, at least, double the execution time and complexity of the form. Also, the signification and salutation are typically only executed in formal situations, such as competitions and tests; otherwise, a form is executed alone – either from the horse stance (the lower forms) or the attention stance (the upper forms).

The next variation is whether the signifying hand touched or hovered over the backstop hand. If the signifying hand was touching the backstop hand, this indicated that the form being executed was modified from the standard execution. But, if the signifying hand hovered over the backstop hand, this indicated that the form was to be executed without modification. The exceptions to this rule are the forms five and six. The forms five and six would always have the signifying hand touch the backstop hand.

Another variation is to signify on both sides of the body or just a single side. Signifying on a single side of the body indicated that the form would be executed on only that side. For instance, if the signification was only given on the right side, then only the right side of the form would be executed. But, if given on both sides of the body, then both the left and right side of the form would be executed. This variation is specifically indicative of Short Form One - which is commonly executed on both the right and left side for competition.

Chapter 4 - Execution of Long Form One

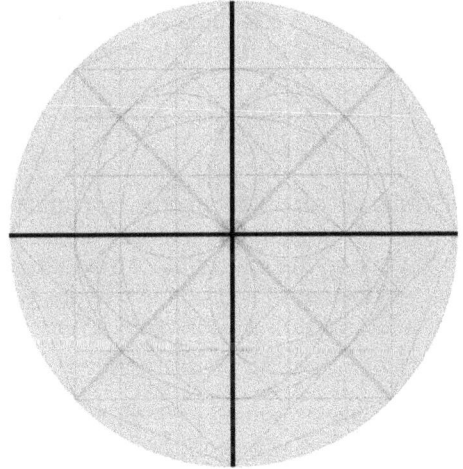

In this section, we will discuss the execution of Long Form One. The execution presented, for the purposes of this discussion, will be considered the standard execution of the form. All information about the form will be derived from this standard of execution. This does not mean there are not legitimate variations to this standard.

Variations can be classified into two major groups: permanent and non-permanent. Non-permanent variations are variations that are made to a form for a specific purpose, such as for competition or for demonstration. Permanent variations are variations that are consciously or mistakenly made to a form, but ultimately end up being a permanent change to the standard execution of a form.

Non-permanent variations can be defined as any variation from the standard that is made to a form for any specific purpose - without the intent of changing the system of American Kenpo. In other words, this type of variation is made to a form without wanting to teach this variation as a "new" way of executing the standard form. Rather, it is executed and / or taught for a specific purpose: such as for tournament competition.

Permanent variations can be broken down into two types: destructive and non-destructive.

Destructive variations can be defined as a variation that detracts from or eliminates some information that is intended to be demonstrated during the execution of the form. This can include: missing maneuvers, altered maneuvers, and / or improperly executed maneuvers. Because of this destructive variations should be avoided and eliminated.

Non-destructive variations can be defined as a variation that changes the form in some way, but does not interfere with the information that is intended to be demonstrated during the execution of the form. These variations are completely acceptable, but should be noted as a variation from the standard.

Non-Permanent Variations

Non-permanent variations usually arise from a specific need. This need usually revolves around demonstration of the form for others - either for a special occasion, demonstration, and / or for competition. Usually, these types of variations are done for the purpose of: visually enhancing, extending the length of, or impressing a specific intended audience (i.e. judges, spectators, visitors, etc.). This type of variation can be a "one time" variation or may become a personally "permanent" variation. Either way, the end result is the same: it is not the intent of these types of variations to replace the standard execution of the base form - rather to be executed in addition to the base form.

One cautionary note should be highlighted about these types of variations: they sometimes become permanent variations. This should be avoided. Why this happens usually arises from either mis-communication and / or laziness. Either a student learned the form with the variation(s) and just assumed that this was the standard and / or just liked the variation better and used it to replace the standard. Not knowing (and / or not caring) that the variation was never intended to be permanent.

Because these types of variations are so diverse, it is hard to list and / or classify them. They can range from simply executing the stances extremely low, to splicing forms together, to changing the base form to the point where it is almost unrecognizable.

Non-Destructive Variations

Because Long Form One adds complexity over Short Form One, it, by definition, adds areas in which the form can be varied. This section lists a few of the common non-destructive variations that are commonly taught.

Some instructors teach kia's with the execution of the punches and at other places throughout the form. Most do not.

Many instructors teach the timing between the block / punch sequence in the first section of the form be executed with the same time gap - i.e. 1-2. Many instructors teach the timing should emphasize the power of the punch - i.e. 1...2.

Most instructors teach that the triple block section should be executed with a timing gap between each group of blocks - i.e. 1-2-3...4-5-6...7-8-9...etc. But, some instructors teach that the triple block section should be executed with a regular beat - i.e. 1-2-3-4-5-6-7-8-9-etc.

Most instructors teach the timing of the isolation execution with a regular beat - with each maneuver of the isolation given the same time span - i.e. 1-2-3-4-5-6-7-8-9-etc. Yet, some instructors teach the timing with a time gap between each grouped maneuver - i.e. 1-2-3...4-5-6...7-8-9...etc. And, still others differ the timing gaps between the blocks and the punches.

Many instructors teach that the blocks and punches of the isolation should be executed looking straight ahead. While other instructors insist that one should look at what they are punching and therefore look in the direction of each punch. While looking is perfectly acceptable, turning from the horse is not. Turning, by definition, eliminates the horse, and breaks the definition of an isolation; and therefore should be avoided.

Execution of Long Form One

As one can clearly see, in Long Form One, timing seems to be the most common type of variation to the form. This is due to the fact that the form is still not very complex, and the timing is a simple 1-in-1 beat.

One other common type of variation also needs to be mentioned. These are variations that are not considered to be permanent,

Various "Standards"

As a general rule, all American Kenpo forms will have various "correct" ways of execution. This is due to a number of factors. But, each factor can be whittled down to one common and important characteristic, they each effect the "standard" execution of the form. Now, carry any of these change factors out a couple of instructor-to-student generations, and you get a resulting form with variations from the beginning of the cycle. But, each generation will swear that they do the form correctly. And, in their mind they are correct. Who is to say otherwise?

Why is the word "standard" in quotes in this section? Because standardization, as it relates to American Kenpo, can be a relative thing. Even Mr. Parker would change the execution of various forms for various reasons. Most of the time for one demonstration, but sometimes permanently.

For example, American Kenpo, as a style that we recognize today, was developed and evolved over a number of decades. During this time, SGM Parker got a large amount of feedback from a great number of direct and indirect students. Whenever he found feedback that was sound and reasonable, he would roll that feedback into his system. But, doing so would leave a number of students that were already taught the form with a slight variation from the now current "standard." Granted, this was infrequent, but it did happen. As far as this relates to Long Form One all changes to the form had completely stopped by the early to mid 1960's.

Execution of Long Form One　71

Another reason for alternate "standards" of a form is that Mr. Parker would sometimes vary a form slightly while teaching it to a specific individual. This is called giving the form a signature. This practice was done so that when a new individual would come to Mr. Parker making claims as to their lineage, Mr. Parker could "test" the individual by having them perform a single or series of forms. From what he saw, SGM Parker could determine whether or not they were being truthful. With this knowledge, he could quickly determine the relative reliability of the individual. But, this practice has a serious side effect - the signature became a "standard." Why? Because that is how the practitioner learned the form from SGM Parker; and, the individual can correctly say that SGM Parker taught them to do the form that specific way. And, they are correct.

A third reason for a "standard" is the, "doesn't effect the information in the form" reason. This comes about because American Kenpo forms can be considered "books" of information about the system. But, certain moves and/or maneuvers can be altered slightly without information being lost or altered in the form. These changes are considered acceptable to the instructor, and as a new generation is taught the form, they will learn it slightly different from the previous generation, generally without any information about the original version and reason for the change.

Probably the most common reason for a "standard" comes about from human error. The scenario goes like this: Mr. Parker teaches a student a form. The person goes home and practices the form, but forgets or accidentally varies the form in some way. But, they never get any further correction and/or feedback from SGM Parker about the "new" way of doing the form. They now teach it to a student with the change, each believing it is the correct and original way of executing the form. And, the cycle continues.

Form Standard Execution

Note:
 H = Horizontal - Example: 6:00H
 V = Vertical - Example 12:00V

From a meditating horse stance...

1
Step back with your left foot (toward 6:00H) into a right neutral bow (facing 12:00H) with a right, hammering, inward block (toward 10:30H) (defending 12:00H) (major) while simultaneously retracting (toward 6:00H) your left arm to a left chambered position, palm up (toward 12:00V).

2
Pivot forward (toward 12:00H) (clockwise H) into a right forward bow (facing 12:00H) with a left, thrusting, straight punch (toward 12:00H) (major) while simultaneously retracting (toward 6:00H) your right arm to a right chambered position, palm up (toward 12:00V).

3
Draw your right foot toward your left foot (toward 6:00H) into a transitory, right, 45 degree, cat stance (facing 12:00H) with a right, thrusting, inward, cover block (toward 10:30H) (defending 12:00H) (minor) while simultaneously retracting (toward 6:00H) your left arm to a left chambered position, palm up (toward 12:00V).

© 2014 EPAKS Publications

Execution of Long Form One 73

Note: This transitory maneuver (highlighted maneuver) is executed with the same timing as the other non-transitory maneuvers in this form - i.e. the motion is paused in the middle (intersection position) of the transitory maneuver. Unlike the other transitory maneuvers in this form which do not pause the motion during the execution of the transitory maneuver.

4
Complete the right, reverse, step through (toward 6:00H) into a left neutral bow (facing 12:00H) with a left, thrusting, inward block (toward 1:30H) (defending 12:00H) (major) while simultaneously retracting (toward 6:00H) your right arm to a right chambered position, palm up (toward 12:00V).

5
Pivot forward (toward 12:00H) (counter-clockwise H) into a left forward bow toward (facing 12:00H) with a right, thrusting, straight punch (toward 12:00H) (major) while simultaneously retracting (toward 6:00H) your left arm to a left chambered position, palm up (toward 12:00V).

6a
Cover (90 degree) step with your right foot (toward 3:00H) (counter-clockwise H), into a transitory, left, neutral bow (facing 9:00H) with a transitory, right, thrusting, inward, cover block (toward 7:30H) (defending 9:00H) (minor) while simultaneously retracting (toward 3:00H) your left arm to a left chambered position, palm up (toward 12:00V).

6b
Settle into a left neutral bow (facing 9:00H) with a left, thrusting, vertical, outward block (toward 6:00H) (defending 9:00H) (major) while simultaneously retracting (toward 3:00H) your right arm to a right chambered position, palm up (toward 12:00V).

7
Pivot forward (toward 9:00H) (counter-clockwise H) into a left forward bow (facing 9:00H) with a right thrusting straight punch (toward 9:00H) (major) while simultaneously retracting (toward 3:00H) your left arm to a left chambered position, palm up (toward 12:00V).

8a
Draw your left foot toward your right foot (toward 3:00H) into a transitory, left, 45 degree, cat stance (facing 9:00H) with a left, thrusting, inward, cover block (toward 10:30H) (defending 9:00H) (minor) while simultaneously retracting (toward 3:00H) your right arm to a right chambered position, palm up (toward 12:00V).

8b
Complete the left, reverse, step through (toward 3:00H) into a right neutral bow (facing 9:00H) with a right, thrusting, vertical, outward block (toward 12:00H) (defending 9:00H) (major) while simultaneously retracting (toward 3:00H) your left arm to a left chambered position, palm up (toward 12:00V).

© 2014 EPAKS Publications

Execution of Long Form One

9
Pivot forward (toward 9:00H) into a right forward bow (facing 9:00H) with a left, thrusting, straight punch (toward 9:00H) (major) while simultaneously retracting (toward 3:00H) your right arm to a right chambered position, palm up (toward 12:00V).

10a
Cover (180 degree) step with your right foot (toward 6:00H) (counter-clockwise H) into a transitory, left, reverse bow (facing 3:00H) while having both your left and right arms remain in place.

10b
Immediately pivot (counter-clockwise H) into a left, offset, fighting horse (facing 3:00H) with the execution of a left, outward, thrusting, horizontal elbow strike (toward 3:00H) (major).

10c
Lower (anchor) your left elbow (toward 6:00V) to your left hip in preparation for the next maneuver.
Note: The above move is executed in order to achieve a greater path of travel for the left upward block (the next maneuver) and is accomplished by using the left fist as the primary pivot point.

10d
Pivot forward (toward 3:00H) (clockwise H) into a left neutral bow (facing 3:00H) with a left, thrusting, upward block (toward 3:00H) (toward 12:00V) (major).

11
Pivot forward (toward 3:00H) into a left forward bow (facing 3:00H) with a right, thrusting, straight punch (toward 3:00H) (major) while simultaneously retracting (toward 9:00H) your left arm to a left chambered position, palm up (toward 12:00V).

12a
Draw your left foot toward your right foot (toward 9:00H) into a transitory, left, 45 degree, cat stance (facing 3:00H) with a left, thrusting, inward, cover block (toward 4:30H) (minor) while simultaneously retracting (toward 9:00H) your right arm to a right chambered position, palm up (toward 12:00V).

12b
Complete the left, reverse, step through (toward 9:00H) into a right neutral bow (facing 3:00H) with a right, thrusting, upward block (toward 9:00H) (toward 12:00V) (major), while simultaneously retracting your left arm to a left chambered position, palm up (toward 12:00H).

13
Pivot forward (toward 3:00H) into a right forward bow (facing 3:00H) with a left, thrusting, straight punch (toward 3:00H) (major) while simultaneously retracting (toward 9:00H) your right arm to a right chambered position, palm up (toward 12:00V).

14a
Cover (90 degree) step with your right foot (toward 6:00H) (clockwise H) into a transitory, right, neutral bow (facing 6:00H) with a left, inside-downward, palm up (toward 12:00V), cover block (toward 9:00H) (defending 6:00H) (minor) while simultaneously cocking your right arm horizontally across your body (toward 3:00H) to your left upper hip area, palm up (toward 12:00V).

© 2014 EPAKS Publications

14b
Settle (toward 6:00V) into a right neutral bow (facing 6:00H) with a right, hammering, outside-downward, palm down (toward 6:00V) block (toward 9:00H) (defending 6:00H) (major) while simultaneously retracting (toward 12:00H) your left arm to a left chambered position, palm up (toward 12:00V).

15
Pivot forward (toward 6:00H) (clockwise H) into a right forward bow (facing 6:00H) with a left, thrusting, straight punch (toward 6:00H) (major) while simultaneously retracting (toward 12:00H) your right arm to a right chambered position, palm up (toward 12:00V).

16a
Draw your right foot toward your left foot (toward 12:00H) into a transitory, right, 45 degree, cat stance (facing 6:00H) with a right, inside-downward, palm up (toward 12:00V), cover block (toward 9:00H) (defending 6:00H) (minor) while simultaneously cocking your left arm horizontally across your body (toward 9:00H) to your right upper hip area, palm up (toward 12:00V).

16b
Complete the right, reverse, step through (toward 12:00V) into a left neutral bow (facing 6:00H) with a left, hammering, outside-downward, palm down (toward 6:00V) block (toward 3:00H) (defending 6:00H) (major) while simultaneously retracting (toward 12:00H) your right arm to a right chambered position, palm up (toward 12:00V).

17
Pivot forward (toward 6:00H) (clockwise H) into a left forward bow (facing 6:00H) with a right, thrusting, straight punch (toward 6:00H) (major) while simultaneously retracting (toward 12:00H) your left arm to a left chambered position, palm up (toward 12:00V).

© 2014 EPAKS Publications

Note: Throughout the execution of the next section of the form, all modified forward bows will be executed by shifting only the upper part of your body while maintaining your feet in a neutral bow position.

18
Pivot backward (toward 12:00H) (clockwise H) into a left neutral bow (facing 6:00H) with a left, thrusting, inward block (toward 7:30H) (defending 6:00H) (major) while simultaneously retracting (toward 12:00H) your right arm to a right chambered position, palm up (toward 12:00V).

19
Pivot forward (toward 6:00H) (counter-clockwise H) into a left, modified, forward bow (facing 6:00H) with a right, thrusting, inward block (toward 4:30H) (defending 6:00H) (major) while simultaneously retracting (toward 12:00H) your left arm to a left chambered position palm up (toward 12:00V).

20
Pivot backward (toward 12:00H) (clockwise H) into a left neutral bow (facing 6:00H) with a left, thrusting, inward block (toward 7:30H) (defending 6:00H) (major) while simultaneously retracting (toward 12:00H) your right arm to a right chambered position, palm up (toward 12:00V).

© 2014 EPAKS Publications

Execution of Long Form One

21
Left step-through reverse (toward 12:00H) into a right neutral bow (facing 6:00H) with a right, thrusting, inward block (toward 4:30H) (defending 6:00H) (major) while simultaneously retracting (toward 12:00H) your left arm to a left chambered position, palm up (toward 12:00V).

22
Pivot forward (toward 6:00H) (clockwise H) into a right, modified, forward bow (facing 6:00H) with a left, thrusting, inward block (toward 7:30H) (defending 6:00H) (major) while simultaneously retracting (toward 12:00H) your right arm to a right chambered position, palm up (toward 12:00V).

23
Pivot backward (toward 12:00H) (counter-clockwise H) into a right neutral bow (facing 6:00H) with a right, thrusting, inward block (toward 4:30H) (defending 6:00H) (major) while simultaneously retracting (toward 12:00H) your left arm to a left chambered position, palm up (toward 12:00V).

24a
Cover (90 degree) step with your left foot (toward 3:00H) (clockwise H) into a transitory, right, neutral bow (facing 9:00H) with a left, thrusting, inward, cover block (toward 10:30H) (defending 9:00H) (minor) while simultaneously retracting your right arm to a right chambered position, palm up (toward 12:00V).

24b
Settle (toward 6:00V) into a right neutral bow (facing 9:00H) with a right, thrusting, vertical, outward block (toward 12:00H) (defending 9:00H) (major) while simultaneously retracting (toward 3:00H) your left arm to a left chambered position, palm up (toward 12:00V).

25
Pivot forward (toward 9:00H) (clockwise H) into a right, modified, forward bow (facing 9:00H) with a left, thrusting, vertical, outward block (toward 6:00H) (defending 9:00H) (major) while simultaneously retracting (toward 3:00H) your right arm to a right chambered position, palm up (toward 12:00V).

26
Pivot backward (toward 3:00H) (counter-clockwise H) into a right neutral bow (facing 9:00H) with a right, thrusting, vertical, outward block (toward 12:00H) (defending 9:00H) (major) while simultaneously retracting (toward 3:00H) your left arm to a left chambered position, palm up (toward 12:00V).

27a
Right step-through reverse (toward 3:00H) into a left, transitory, neutral bow (facing 9:00H) with a right, thrusting, inward, cover block (toward 7:30H) (defending 9:00H) (minor) while simultaneously retracting (toward 3:00H) your left arm to a left chambered position, palm up (toward 12:00V).

27b
Settle (toward 6:00V) into a left neutral bow (facing 9:00H) with a left, thrusting, vertical, outward block (toward 6:00H) (defending 9:00H) (major) while simultaneously retracting (toward 3:00H) your right arm to a right chambered position, palm up (toward 12:00V).

Execution of Long Form One   81

28
Pivot forward (toward 9:00H) (counter-clockwise H) into a left, modified, forward bow (facing 9:00H) with a right, thrusting, vertical, outward block (toward 12:00H) (defending 9:00H) (major) while simultaneously retracting (toward 3:00H) your left arm to a left chambered position, palm up (toward 12:00V).

29
Pivot backward (toward 3:00H) (clockwise H) into a left neutral bow (facing 9:00H) with a left, thrusting, vertical, outward block (toward 6:00H) (defending 9:00H) (major) while simultaneously retracting (toward 3:00H) your right arm to a right chambered position, palm up (toward 12:00V).

30a
Cover (180 degree) step with your left foot (toward 12:00H) (clockwise) into a transitory, right, neutral bow (facing 3:00H) with a left, thrusting, inward, cover block (toward 4:30H) (defending 3:00H) (minor) while simultaneously retracting (toward 9:00H) your right arm to a right chambered position, palm up (toward 12:00V).

30b
Settle (toward 6:00V) into a right neutral bow (facing 3:00H) with a right, thrusting, upward block (toward 3:00H) (toward 12:00V) (major) while simultaneously retracting (toward 9:00H) your left arm to a left chambered position, palm up (toward 12:00).

31
Pivot forward (toward 3:00H) (clockwise H) into a right, modified, forward bow (facing 3:00H) with a left, thrusting, upward block (toward 3:00H) (toward 12:00V) (major) while simultaneously retracting (toward 9:00H) your right arm to a right chambered position, palm up (toward 12:00V).

© 2014 EPAKS Publications

32
Pivot backward (toward 9:00H) (counter-clockwise H) into a right neutral bow (facing 3:00H) with a right, thrusting, upward block (toward 3:00H) (toward 12:00V) (major) while simultaneously retracting (toward 9:00H) your left arm to a left chambered position, palm up (toward 12:00V).

33a
Right step-through reverse (toward 9:00H) into a left, transitory, neutral bow (facing 3:00H) with a right, thrusting, inward, cover block (toward 1:30H) (defending 3:00H) (minor) while simultaneously retracting (toward 9:00H) your left arm to a left chambered position, palm up (toward 12:00V).

33b
Settle (toward 6:00V) into a left neutral bow (facing 3:00H) with a left, thrusting, upward block (toward 3:00H) (toward 12:00V) (major) while simultaneously retracting (toward 9:00H) your right arm to a right chambered position, palm up (toward 12:00V).

34
Pivot forward (toward 3:00H) (counter-clockwise H) into a left, modified, forward bow (facing 3:00H) with a right, thrusting, upward block (toward 3:00H) (toward 12:00V) (major) while simultaneously retracting (toward 9:00H) your left arm to a left chambered position, palm up (toward 12:00V).

35
Pivot backward (toward 9:00H) (clockwise H) into a left neutral bow (facing 3:00H) with a left, thrusting, upward block (toward 3:00H) (toward 12:00V) (major) while simultaneously retracting (toward 9:00H) your right arm to a right chambered position, palm up (toward 12:00V).

Execution of Long Form One 83

36a
Cover (90 degree) step with your right foot (toward 6:00H) (counter-clockwise H) into a transitory, left, neutral bow (facing 12:00H) with a hammering, right, inside-downward, palm up (toward 12:00V), cover block (toward 9:00H) (defending 12:00H) (minor) while simultaneously maintaining the position of your left arm.

36b
Settle (toward 6:00V) into a left neutral bow (facing 12:00H) with a left, hammering, outside-downward, palm down (toward 6:00V) block (toward 9:00H) (defending 12:00H) (major) while simultaneously retracting (toward 6:00H) your right arm to a right chambered position, palm up (toward 12:00V).

37a
Execute a left, thrusting, inside-downward, palm up (toward 12:00V), cover block (toward 3:00H) (defending 12:00H) (minor) while simultaneously cocking (toward 9:00H) your right arm horizontally across your body to your left upper hip area, palm up (toward 12:00V).

37b
Pivot forward (toward 12:00H) (counter-clockwise H) into a right, modified, forward bow (facing 12:00H) with a right, hammering, outside-downward, palm down (toward 6:00V) block (toward 3:00H) (defending 12:00H) (major) while simultaneously retracting (toward 6:00H) your left arm to a left chambered position, palm up (toward 12:00V).

© 2014 EPAKS Publications

38a
Execute a right, thrusting, inside-downward, palm up (toward 12:00V), cover block (toward 9:00H) (defending 12:00H) (minor) while simultaneously cocking (toward 3:00H) your left arm horizontally across your body to your right upper hip area, palm up (toward 12:00V).

38b
Pivot backward (toward 6:00V) (clockwise H) into a left neutral bow (facing 12:00H) with a left, hammering, outside-downward, palm down (toward 6:00V) block (toward 9:00H) (defending 12:00H) (major) while simultaneously retracting (toward 6:00H) your right arm to a right chambered position, palm up (toward 12:00V).

39a
Left step-through reverse (toward 6:00H) into a right, transitory, neutral bow (facing 12:00H) with a left, thrusting, inside-downward, palm up (toward 12:00V) cover block (toward 3:00H) (defending 12:00H) (minor) while simultaneously cocking (toward 9:00H) your right arm horizontally across your body to your left upper hip area, palm up (toward 12:00V).

39b
Settle (toward 6:00V) into a right neutral bow (facing 12:00H) with a right, hammering, outside-downward, palm down (toward 6:00V) block (toward 3:00H) (defending 12:00H) (major) while simultaneously retracting (toward 6:00H) your left arm to a left chambered position, palm up (toward 12:00V).

40a
Execute a right, thrusting, inside-downward, palm up (toward 12:00V), cover block (toward 9:00H) (defending 12:00H) (minor) while simultaneously cocking (toward 3:00H) your left arm horizontally across your body to your right upper hip area, palm up (toward 12:00V).

© 2014 EPAKS Publications

Execution of Long Form One

40b
Pivot forward (toward 12:00H) (clockwise H) into a right, modified, forward bow (facing 12:00H) with a left, hammering, outside-downward, palm down (toward 6:00V) block (toward 9:00H) (defending 12:00H) (major) while simultaneously retracting (toward 6:00H) your right arm to a right chambered position, palm up (toward 12:00V).

41a
Execute a left thrusting, inside-downward, palm up (toward 12:00V), cover block (toward 3:00H) (defending 12:00H) (minor) while simultaneously cocking (toward 9:00H) your right arm horizontally across your body to your left upper hip area, palm up (toward 12:00V).

41b
Pivot backward (toward 6:00H) (counter-clockwise H) into a right neutral bow (toward 12:00) with a right, hammering, outside-downward, palm down (toward 6:00V) block (toward 3:00H) (defending 12:00H) (major) while simultaneously retracting (toward 6:00H) your left arm to a left chambered position, palm up (toward 12:00V).

42
Step forward (toward 10:30H) with your left foot into a horse (facing 12:00H) with a left, thrusting, inside-downward, palm down (toward 6:00V) block (toward 3:00H) (defending 12:00H) (major) while simultaneously retracting (toward 6:00H) your right arm to a right chambered position, palm up (toward 12:00V).

43
Execute a right, thrusting, inside-downward, palm down (toward 6:00V) block (toward 9:00H) (defending 12:00H) (major) while simultaneously retracting (toward 6:00H) your left arm to a left chambered position, palm up (toward 12:00V).

© 2014 EPAKS Publications

44
Execute a left, thrusting, inside-downward, palm down (toward 6:00V) block (toward 3:00H) (defending 12:00H) (major) while simultaneously retracting (toward 6:00H) your right arm to a right chambered position, palm up (toward 12:00V).

45
Execute a right, hammering, inside-downward, palm up (toward 12:00V) block (toward 9:00H) (defending 12:00H) (major) while simultaneously retracting (toward 6:00H) your left arm to a left chambered position, palm up (toward 12:00V).

46
Execute a left, hammering, inside-downward, palm up (toward 12:00V) block (toward 3:00H) (defending 12:00H) (major) while simultaneously retracting right (toward 6:00H) left arm to a right chambered position, palm up (toward 12:0V).

47
Execute a right, hammering, inside-downward, palm up (toward 12:00V) block (toward 9:00H) (defending 12:00H) (major) while simultaneously retracting (toward 6:00H) your left arm to a left chambered position, palm up (toward 12:00V).

48
Execute a left, pressing, push-down block (toward 6:00V) (defending 12:00H) (major), palm down (toward 6:00V), while simultaneously retracting (toward 6:00H) your right arm to a right chambered position, palm up (toward 12:00V).

© 2014 EPAKS Publications

Execution of Long Form One

49
Execute a right, pressing, push-down block (toward 6:00V) (defending 12:00H) (major), palm down (toward 6:00V), while simultaneously retracting (toward 6:00H) your left arm to a left chambered position, palm up (toward 12:00V).

50
Execute a left, pressing, push-down block (toward 6:00V) (defending 12:00H) (major), palm down (toward 6:00V), while simultaneously retracting (toward 6:00H) your right arm to a right chambered position, palm up (toward 12:00V).

51
Execute a right, thrusting, straight punch (toward 12:00H) (major), palm down (toward 6:00V), while simultaneously retracting (toward 6:00H) your left arm to a left chambered position, palm up (toward 12:00V).

52
Execute a left, thrusting, straight punch (toward 12:00H) (major), palm down (toward 6:00V), while simultaneously retracting (toward 6:00H) your right arm to a right chambered position, palm up (toward 12:00V).

53
Execute a right, thrusting, straight punch (toward 10:30H) (major), palm down (toward 6:00V), while simultaneously retracting (toward 6:00H) your left arm to a left chambered position, palm up (toward 12:00V).

© 2014 EPAKS Publications

54
Execute a left, thrusting, straight punch (toward 1:30H) (major), palm down (toward 6:00V), while simultaneously retracting (toward 6:00H) your right arm to a right chambered position, palm up (toward 12:00V).

55
Execute a right, thrusting, straight punch (toward 9:00H) (major), palm down (toward 6:00V), while simultaneously retracting (toward 6:00H) your left arm to a left chambered position, palm up (toward 12:00V).

56
Execute a left, thrusting, straight punch (toward 3:00H) (major), palm down (toward 6:00V), while simultaneously retracting (toward 6:00H your right arm to a right chambered position, palm up (toward 12:00V).

57
Execute a right, thrusting, uppercut punch (toward 12:00H) (toward 1:30V) (major), palm up (toward 12:00V), while simultaneously retracting (toward 6:00H) your left arm to a left chambered position, palm up (toward 12:00V).

58
Execute a left, thrusting, uppercut punch (toward 12:00H) (toward 1:30V) (major), palm up (toward 6:00V), while simultaneously retracting (toward 6:00H) your right arm to a right chambered position, palm up (toward 12:00V).

59
Open and rotate (180 degrees) (clockwise V) your left hand, in place, palm down (toward 4:30V), with a right, torquing (180 degree) (counter-clockwise H) uppercut punch (toward 12:00H) (toward 1:30V) (minor), palm down (toward 7:30V), into the palm of your left open hand (forming the salutation).

Closing salutation...

Form Standard Execution - Illustration

Note: The double factor blocks and associated transitory 45 degree cat stances are not illustrated in this section - even though they are expressly described in the 'Standard Execution' text. This is done purposely for the sake of simplicity.

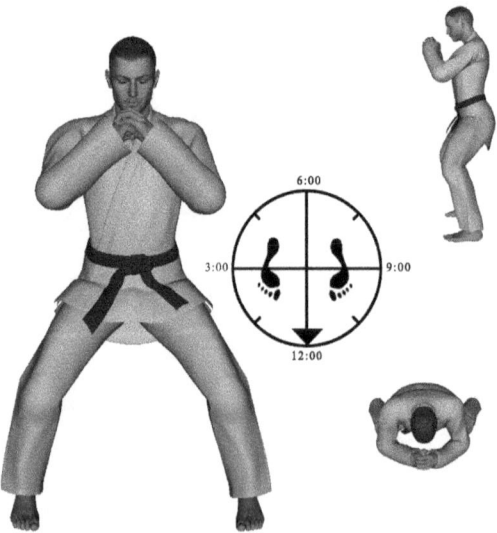

Opening Meditating Horse

Execution of Long Form One

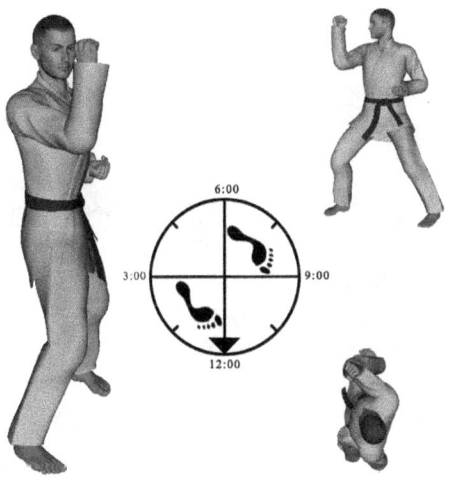

1) Right Hammering Inward Block

2) Left Thrusting Straight Punch

Execution of Long Form One   93

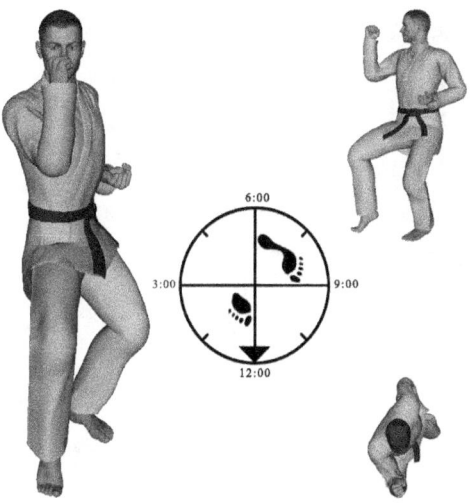

3) Right 45 degree Cat (with right covering inward block)

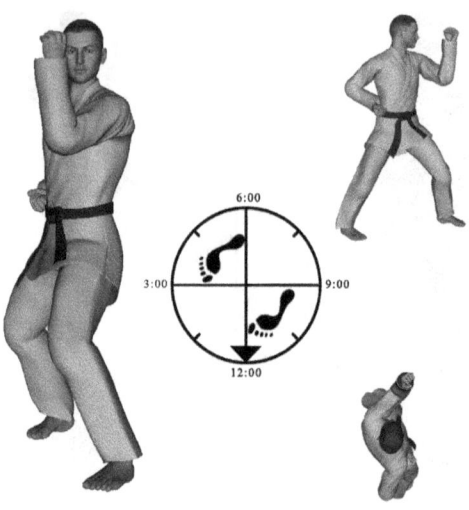

4) Left Thrusting Inward Block

Execution of Long Form One   95

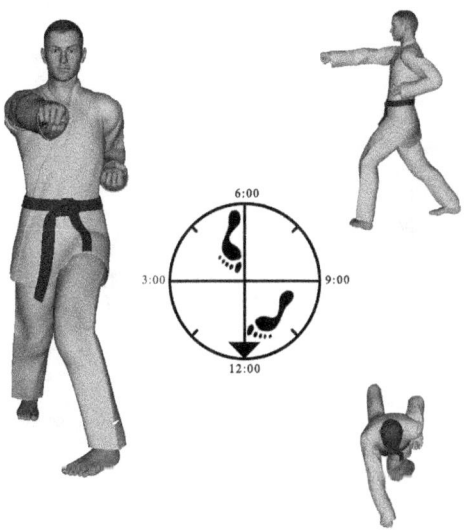

5) Right Thrusting Straight Punch

© 2014 EPAKS Publications

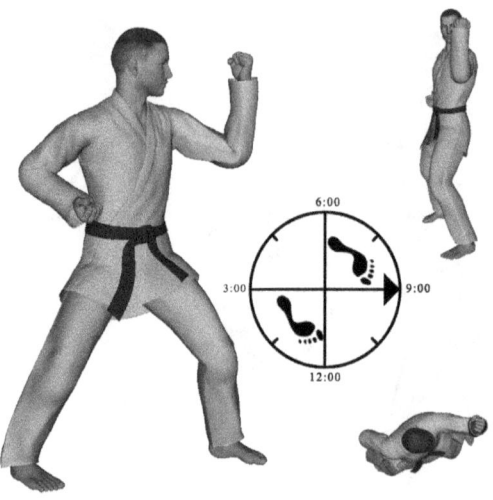

6) Left Vertical Outward Block

Execution of Long Form One 97

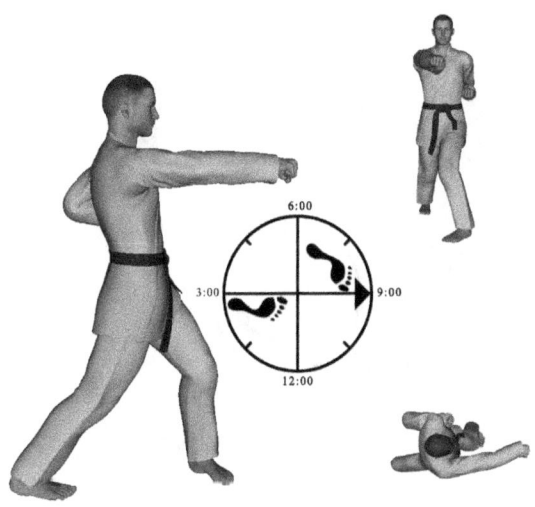

7) Right Thrusting Straight Punch

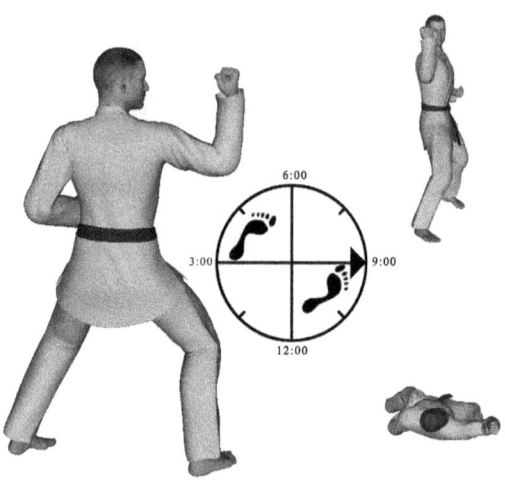

8) Right Vertical Outward Block

Execution of Long Form One — 99

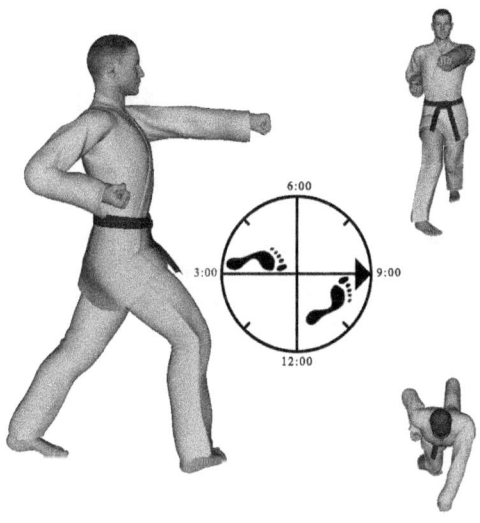

9) Left Thrusting Straight Punch

© 2014 EPAKS Publications

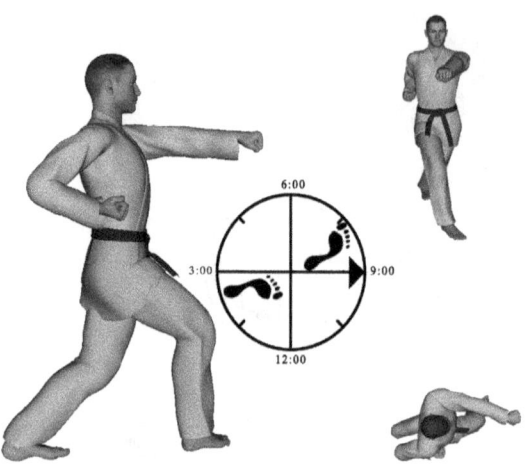

10a) Right Cover Step

Execution of Long Form One | 101

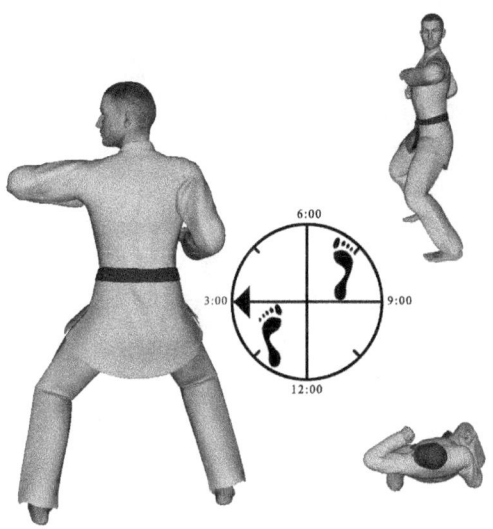

10b) Left Outward Elbow

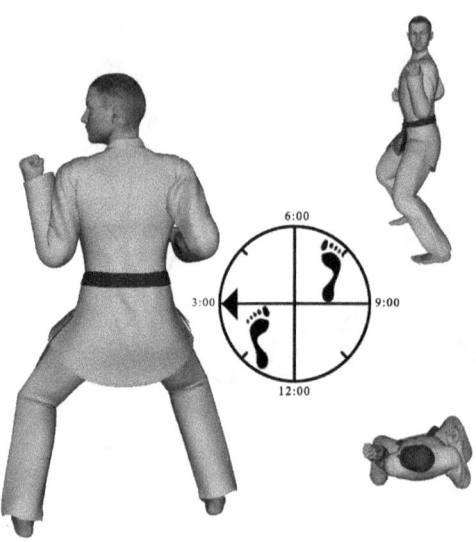

10c) Left Cock (drop of Elbow)

Execution of Long Form One

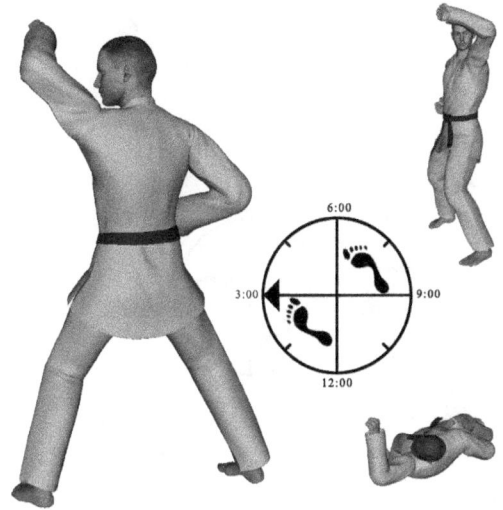

11) Left Upward Block

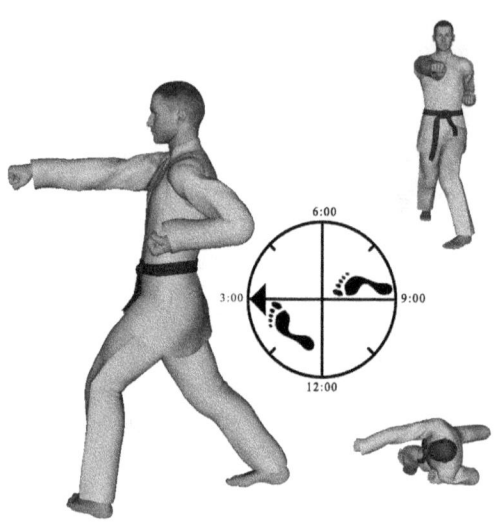

12) Right Thrusting Straight Punch

Execution of Long Form One — 105

13) Right Upward Block

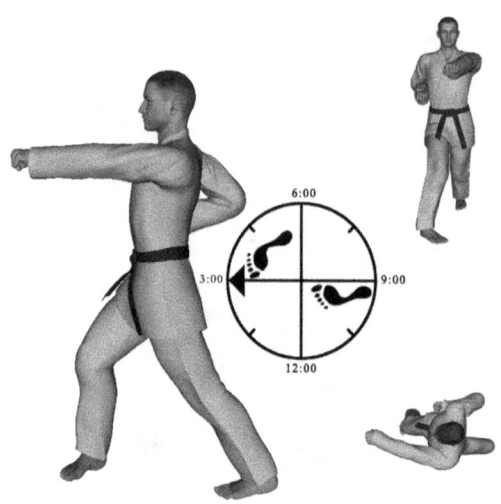

14) Left Thrusting Straight Punch

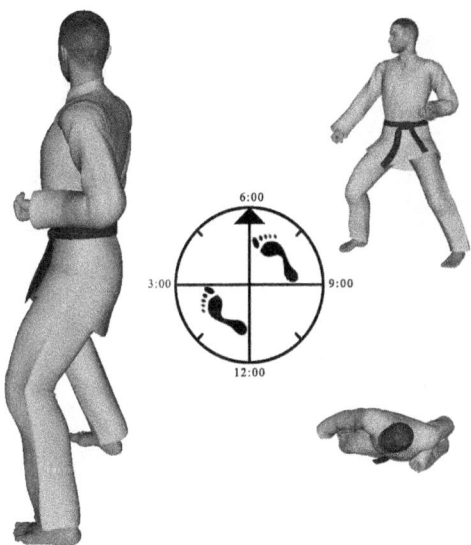

**15) Right Downward Block
(stepping forward toward 6:00H)**

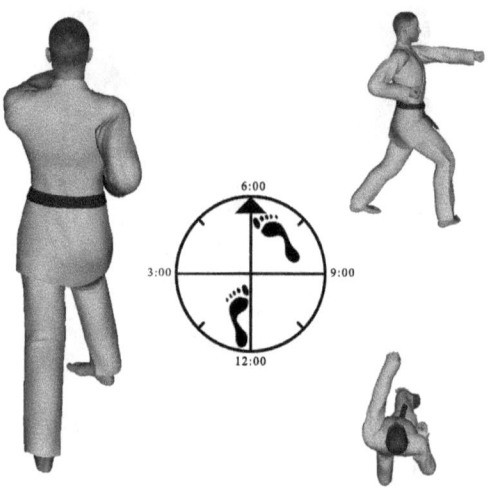

16) Left Thrusting Straight Punch

Execution of Long Form One 109

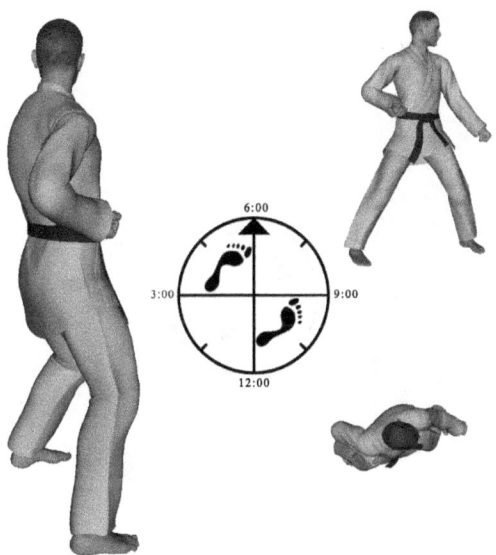

17) Left Downward Block

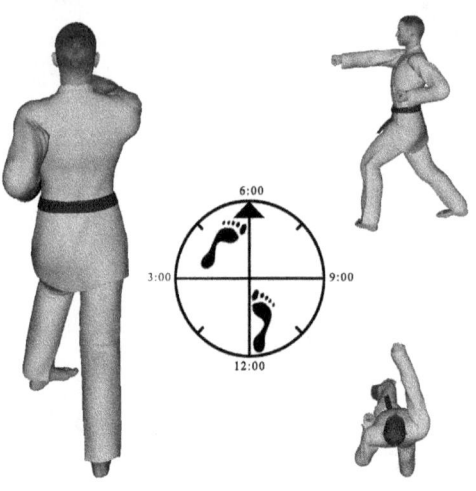

18) Right Thrusting Straight Punch

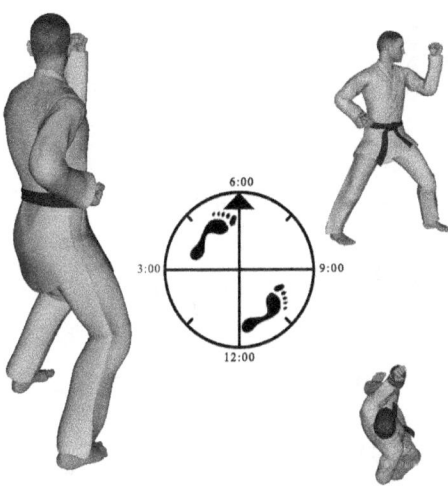

19) Left Inward Block (front arm)

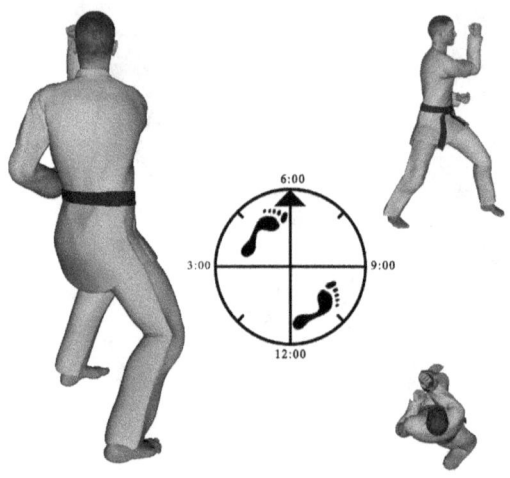

20) Right Inward Block (rear arm)

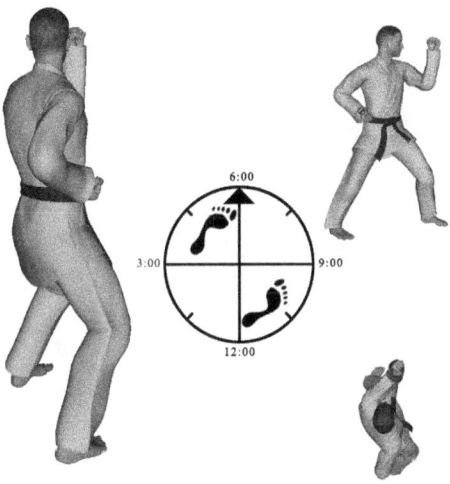

21) Left Inward Block (front arm)

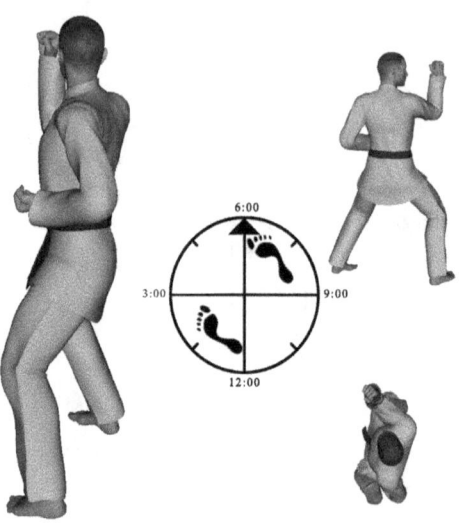

22) Right Inward Block (front arm)

Execution of Long Form One   115

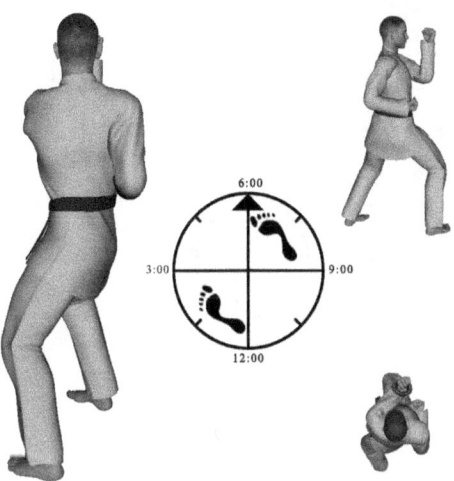

23) Left Inward Block (rear arm)

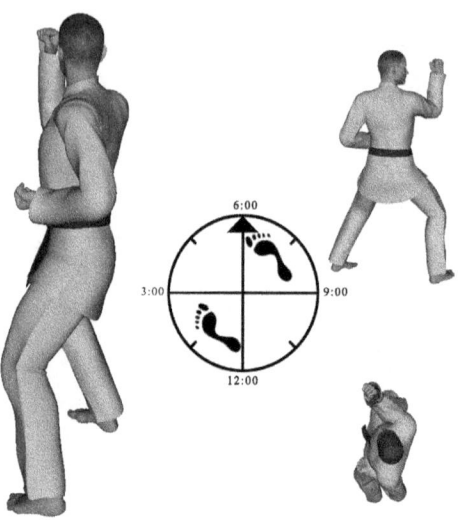

24) Right Inward Block (front arm)

Execution of Long Form One   117

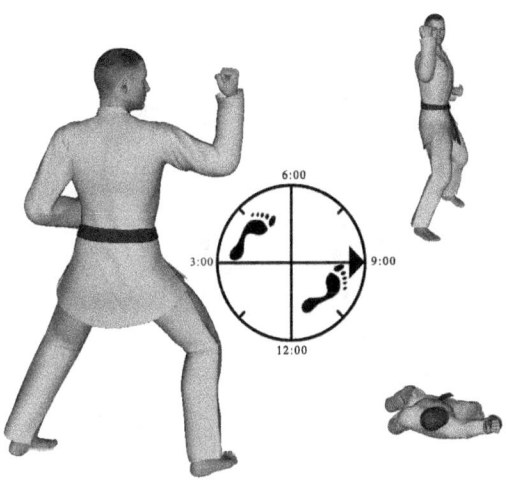

25) Right Outward Block (front arm)

26) Left Outward Block (rear arm)

Execution of Long Form One 119

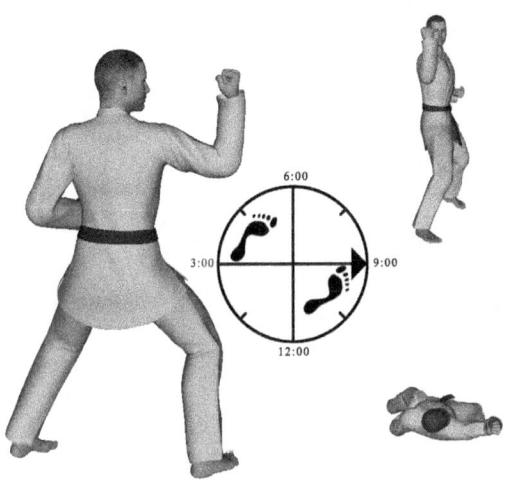

27) Right Outward Block (front arm)

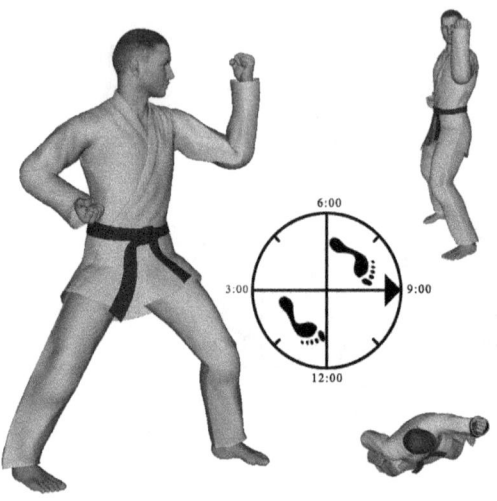

28) Left Outward Block (front arm)

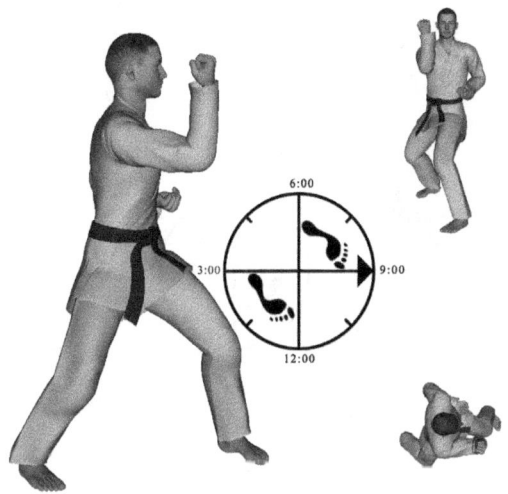

29) Right Outward Block (rear arm)

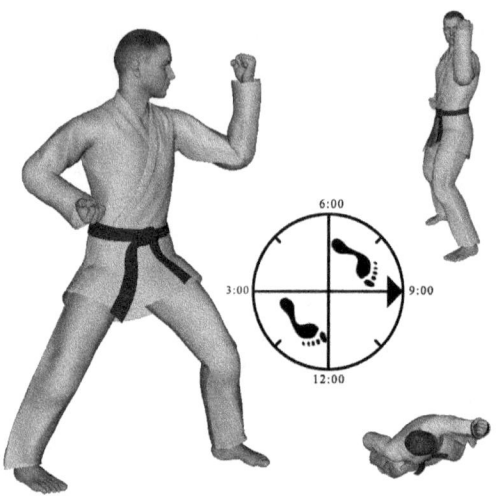

30) Left Outward Block (front arm)

Execution of Long Form One 123

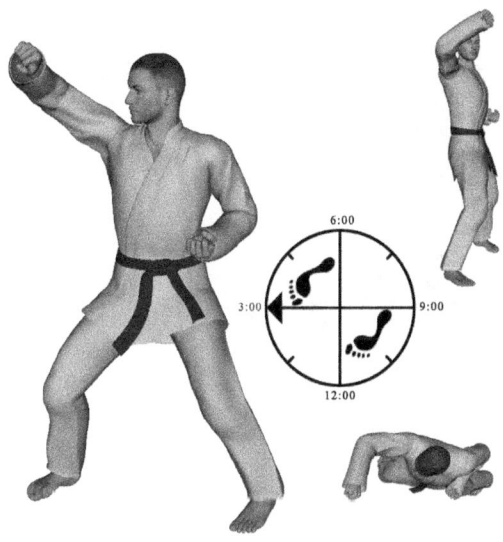

31) Right Upward Block (front arm)

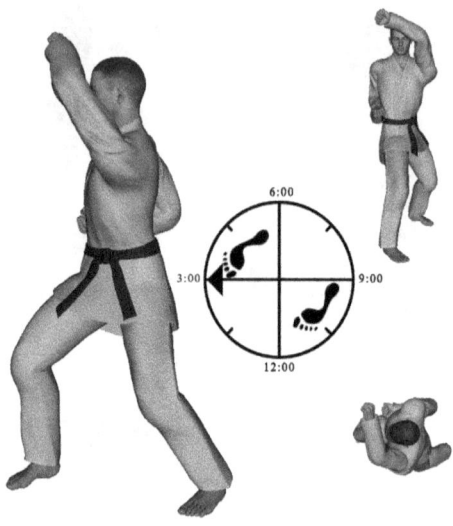

32) Left Upward Block (rear arm)

Execution of Long Form One | 125

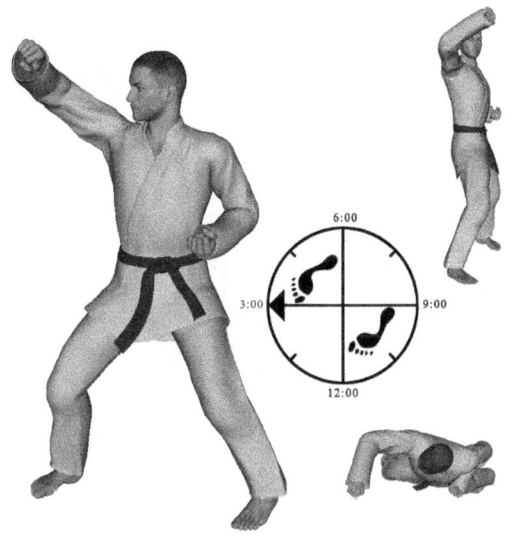

33) Right Upward Block (front arm)

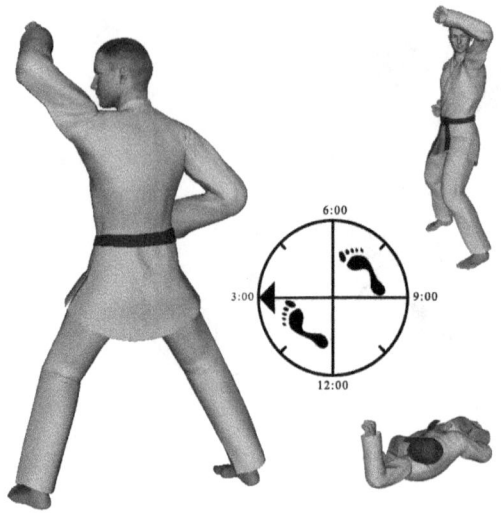

34) Left Upward Block (front arm)

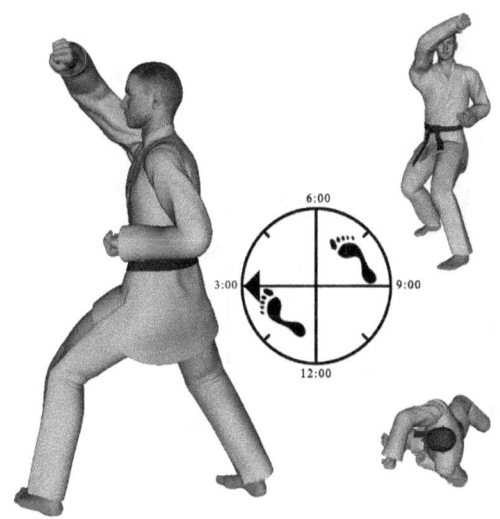

35) Right Upward Block (rear arm)

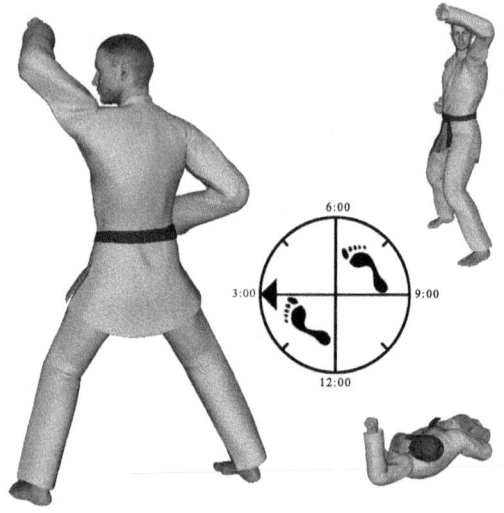

36) Left Upward Block (front arm)

Execution of Long Form One   129

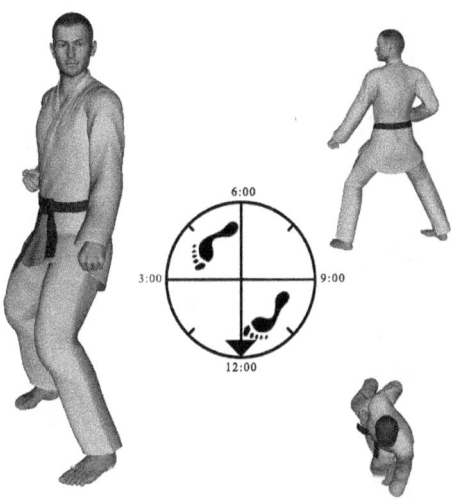

37) Left Downward Block (front arm)

© 2014 EPAKS Publications

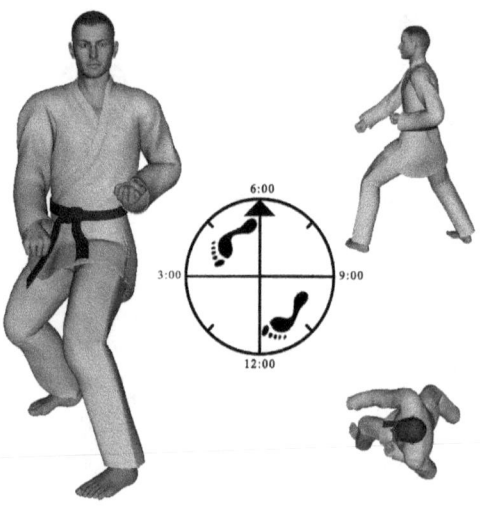

38) Right Downward Block (rear arm)

Execution of Long Form One   131

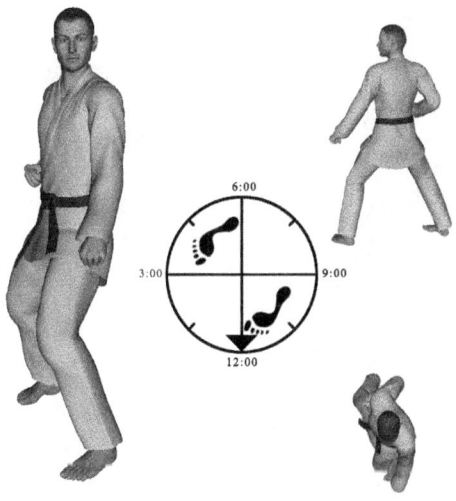

39) Left Downward Block (front arm)

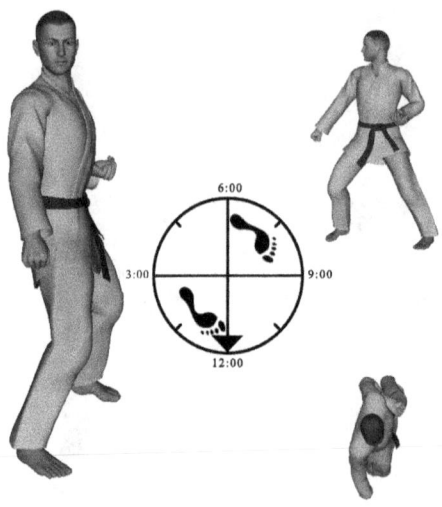

40) Right Downward Block (front arm)

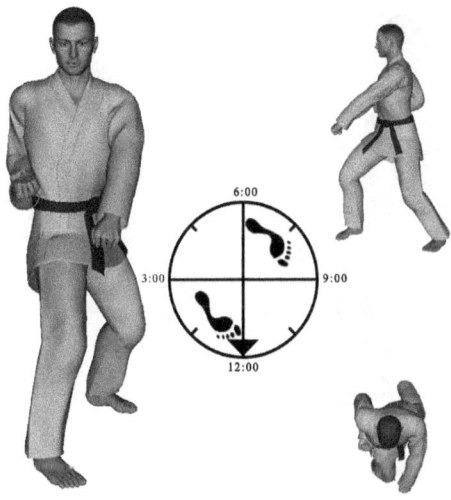

41) Left Downward Block (rear arm)

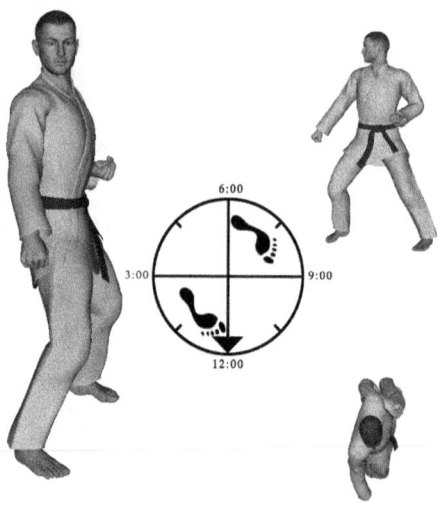

42) Right Downward Block (front arm)

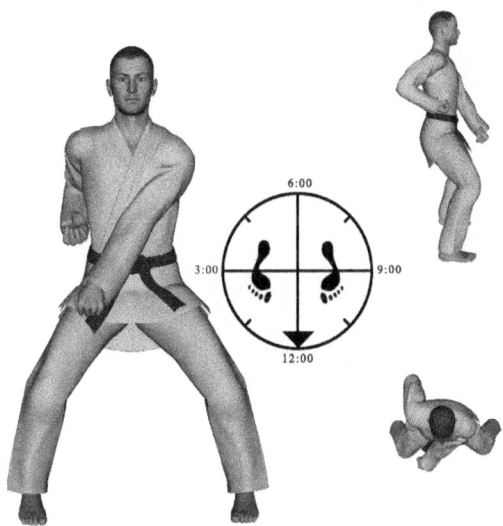

43) Left Inside Downward - Palm Down Block
(with left step forward into Horse Stance)

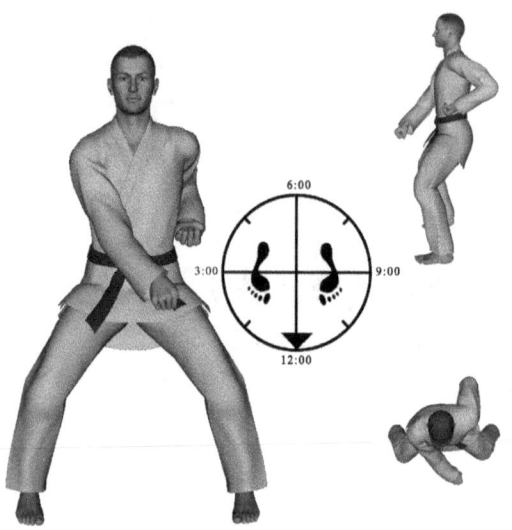

44) Right Inside Downward - Palm Down Block

Execution of Long Form One — 137

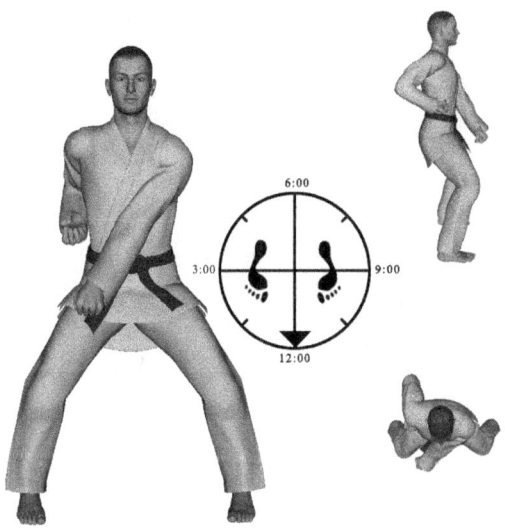

45) Left Inside Downward - Palm Down Block

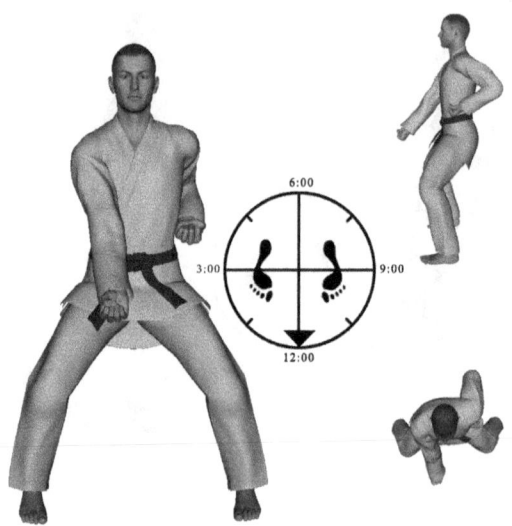

46) Right Inside Downward - Palm Up Block

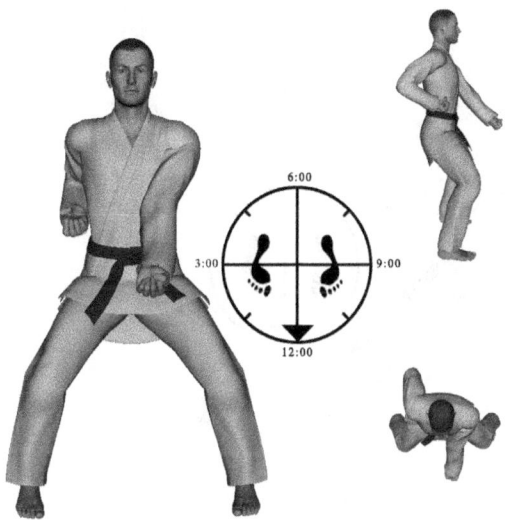

47) Left Inside Downward - Palm Up Block

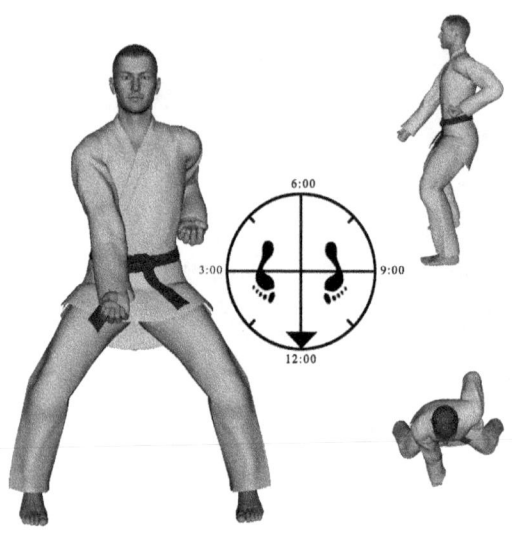

48) Right Inside Downward - Palm Up Block

Execution of Long Form One

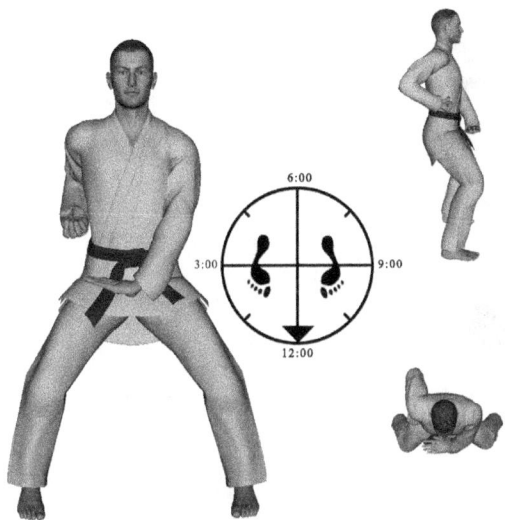

49) Left Push-Down Block

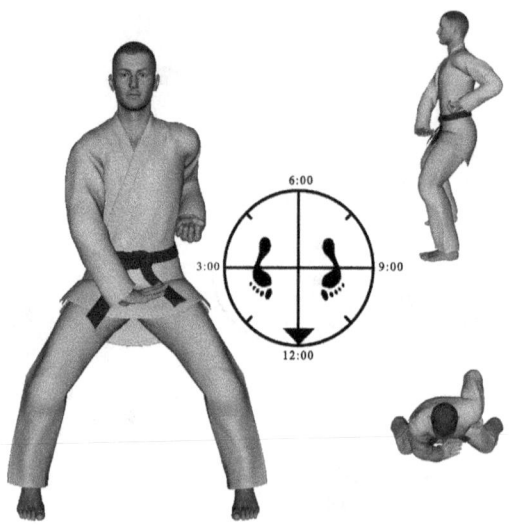

50) Right Push-Down Block

Execution of Long Form One

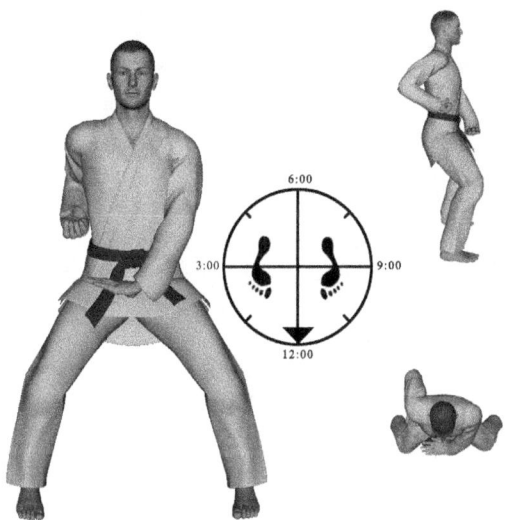

51) Left Push-Down Block

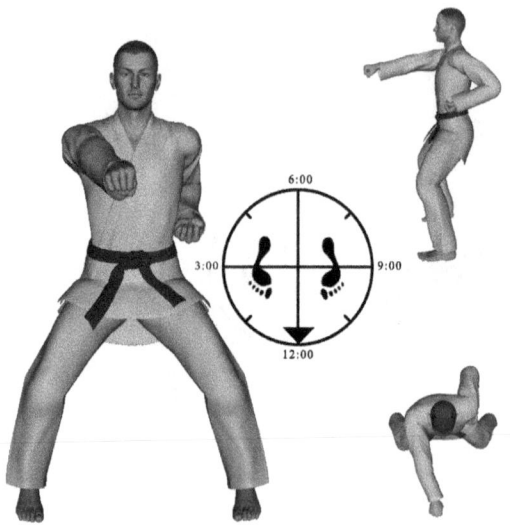

52) Right Straight Punch (12:00H)

Execution of Long Form One 145

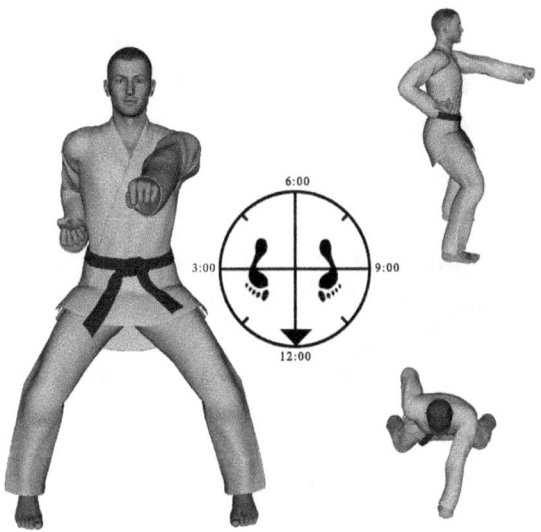

53) Left Straight Punch (12:00H)

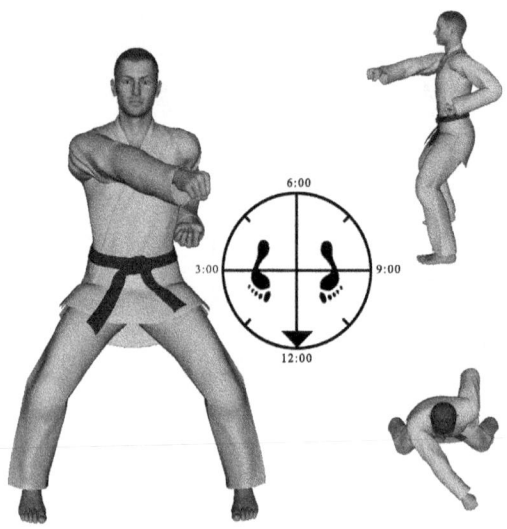

54) Right Straight Punch (10:30H)

Execution of Long Form One — 147

55) Left Straight Punch (1:30H)

© 2014 EPAKS Publications

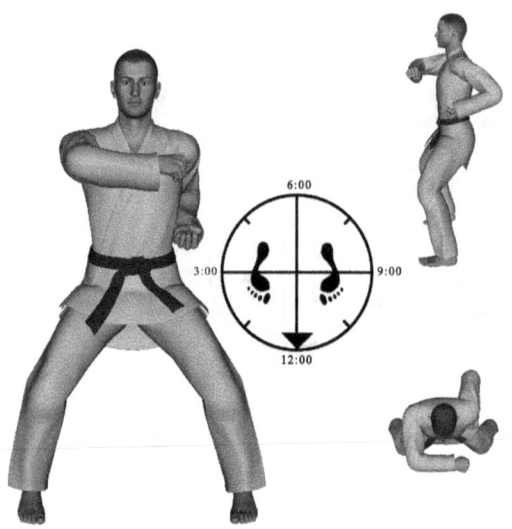

56) Right Straight Punch (9:00H)

Execution of Long Form One 149

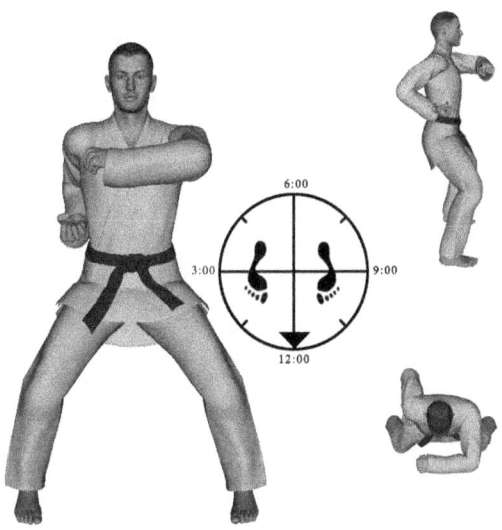

57) Left Straight Punch (3:00H)

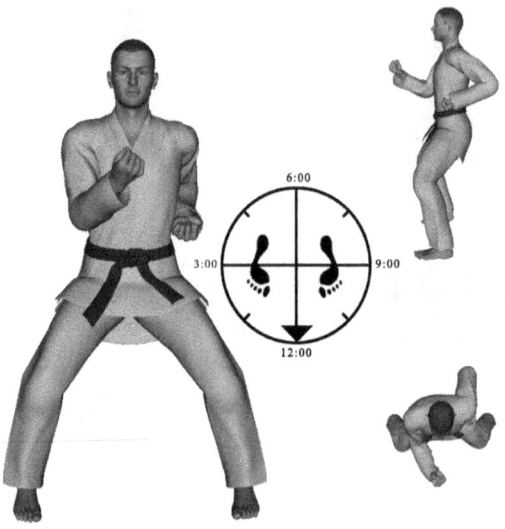

58) Right Uppercut Punch

Execution of Long Form One

59) Left Uppercut Punch

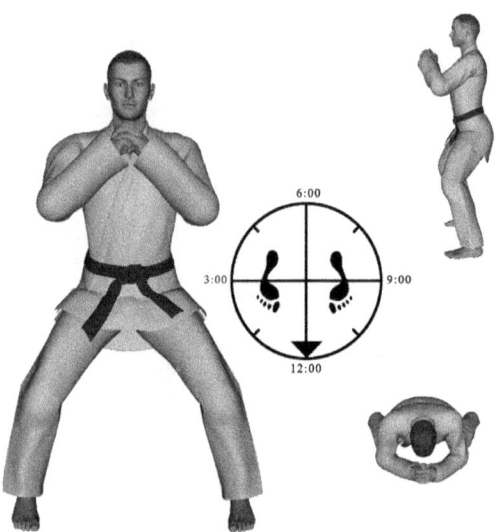

60) bring your right closed fist to meet your left hand to form the closing Meditating Horse

Form Standard Execution - Video

EPAKS has produced a number of videos that have been uploaded to YouTube. The purpose of these videos is to demonstrate the execution of American Kenpo forms and self-defense techniques. They are not intended to be perfect. Instead, they are intended to be reasonably good examples of execution which the viewer can use as a benchmark. Among the videos is one demonstrating Long Form One. It may be viewed here:

http://www.youtube.com/watch?v=VTHoz5ECMiY

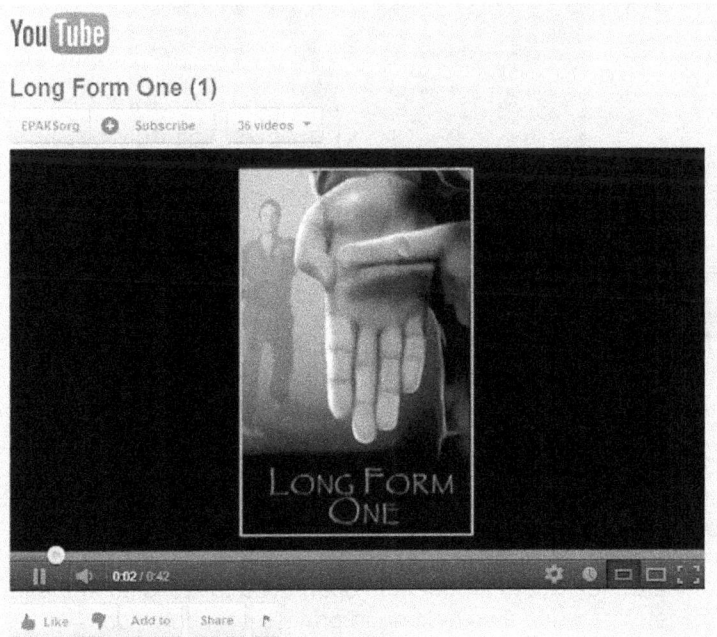

Chapter 5 - Understanding American Kenpo Forms

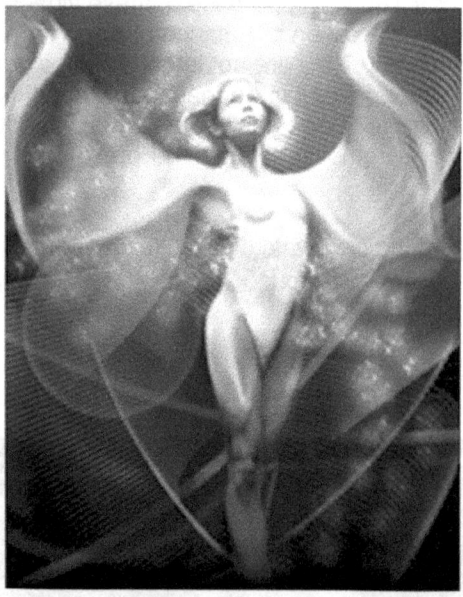

The most important thing to understand about an American Kenpo form is that it should not be thought of as an imaginary fight between the performer and (an) imaginary opponent(s). Many people make the assumption that is the way one must think about American Kenpo forms. This assumption comes from a couple of venues. For one, most self-defense systems structure their forms this way. For another, almost everyone visualizes an opponent in some way while executing their form. Visualization of an opponent is often used to focus strikes and maneuvers while also helping to provide psychological motivation. Also, visualization of an opponent is often used while learning and/or teaching a form.

In contrast to other styles of self-defense, American Kenpo forms are defined as:

A predefined series of maneuvers that:
1) show the rules and principles of motion,
2) that everything has a reverse and an opposite,
3) by giving an example

Another way to look at it is: an American Kenpo form can be thought of as a packet of information, exposed as movement, used to convey some of the information that shapes the framework of the American Kenpo system. This information is to be learned along with the movements, thus continuing an unbroken line of succession from instructor to student.

One common way to begin to understand the information presented in American Kenpo forms is to first break the forms down into their respective categories. Through some simple analysis one of the first things that should begin to become apparent is that their appears to be three different types of forms. This appearance is correct. The name of the concept associated with this observation is called the Dictionary / Encyclopedia / Appendix analogy. Whereas dictionaries define individual words encyclopedias explain things and concepts in greater detail. But, appendices expand and expound upon a small or focused area of information. Using this explanation, one can create a one-to-one correlation to the observed three categories of forms.

The first four forms (the one's and the two's) appear to have a slightly different style than the higher forms. These forms fall into the 'dictionary' category. They are commonly referred to as defining motion. By this it is meant that these forms concentrate more on the basics and demonstrating their opposites and reverses, and less upon the concepts and theories.

The higher forms (the three's and up) appear to be far more complex than the lower forms. These forms fall into the 'encyclopedia' category. These forms, in contrast to the dictionary forms, lean more toward concentrating on the concepts and theories of American Kenpo and less towards the physical opposites and reverses.

The remaining type of form (the set) is very different from all the other forms. Sets are so different, in fact, that they even have a different name - i.e. sets. These forms fall into the 'appendix' category. By this it is meant that these forms have a very narrow scope. In other words, these forms concentrate and explore the information present within specific genre of information/motion.

Understanding Long Form One

So, how does Long Form One fit into the Dictionary / Encyclopedia / Appendix analogy?

First, Long Form One continues and then extends the structure and sequence started by Short Form One. As a matter of fact, all of the forms up through Long Form Two have the same fundamental properties. These are: all Dictionary forms start from a Meditating Horse stance; begin with a Right, Hammering, Inward Block; and work on an In / Out / Up / Down sequence.

Next, Long Form One builds on the foundation which was set in place by Short Form One. Specifically, it extends the demonstration of the concept of opposites (left / right, up / down, in / out, etc) and reverses (inward / outward, clockwise / counter-clockwise, direct rotational / counter rotational, etc). An important thing to notice about Long Form One extending the foundation is that even though the extension is primarily focused on physical motion, it also includes conceptual opposites.

As an example: an opposite to a right block is a left block - physical motions. Whereas an opposite to understanding is not understanding - a concept.

The Design of Long Form One

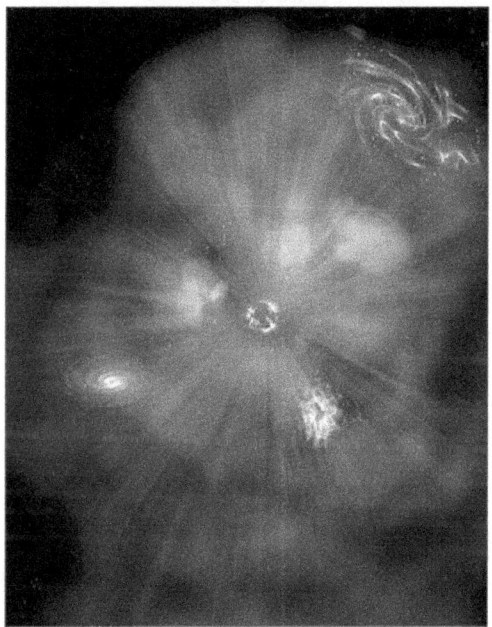

After learning to execute any form in the American Kenpo system, one must begin to consider how the form fits into the design of the system itself. Each form has its place, purpose, and overall contribution to the structure of the American Kenpo system. Long Form One is no exception.

Long Form One's essential purpose and contribution is the continuation of the foundation laid out by Short Form One. As such, it contains all of the movements and concepts Short Form One introduced, but then expands upon both. And, with each new movement comes associated principles, rules, theories, and concepts. Yet, this expansion is done in a very precise and calculated way. Each new movement either has a direct backward link to Short Form One or a direct forward link to one of the other forms in the American Kenpo system (such as Short Form Two) - i.e. there are no extraneous movements.

© 2014 EPAKS Publications

As the overall analysis of Long Form One progresses, one should become keenly aware that this form exemplifies the definition of an American Kenpo form. And as such, the expansion of Short Form One is accomplished by adhering to this definition - not diverging from it.

Why Long Form One?

One of the first things that needs to be considered when beginning to think about Long Form One is why it is called Long Form One. First of all why Form One and why Long?

Why Form One? There already is a Form One - Short Form One. This form could have been named Form Two and Short Form One could have just been named Form One. This naming convention was set in place by SGM Parker because he wanted the practitioner to understand that any Short Form 'x' and any Long Form 'x' are directly related to one another. In other words, they are essentially the same form only with subtle differences and additions. Because of this naming convention of short and long plus the same name (i.e. Form One), the practitioner is always (and obviously) reminded that they are executing forms that are so related to one another that they are given the same name.

Why Short and Long? This part of the naming convention was set in place by SGM Parker because he wanted the practitioner to understand that the short form is fundamentally the shorter version of a long form. By doing this he helped reiterate the fact that the two forms are the same form, but highlighted the fact that the forms are different. And, eluded to the fact that the short form was the foundation form and the long form used that foundation to reiterate and expand upon the information presented in the short form. All with just changing one word from short to long.

Long Form One vs Short Form One

One quick way to begin to think about Long Form One is to compare and contrast it to what is already known. In this case that would be Short Form One. If this comparison is done at a large and general scale, the form can be broken down into three (3) major sections:

1) Short Form One only with Punches and Forward Bows
2) The opposite side of Short Form One only incorporating the back hand block
3) The isolation (i.e. the new material)

Why is this an important way to break down Long Form One? Because it quickly exposes and enunciates some of the fundamental differences and similarities to Short Form One. This break down can then easily be used as a starting point in an analysis of Long Form One. Also, this break down can be used to remember the execution of Long Form One (albeit at a high level) if it is forgotten.

Through this break down it is quickly apparent how Long Form One uses the foundation laid out by Short Form One and then builds upon it. It is also quickly apparent that this extension to the foundation is done primarily through the use of opposites and reverses. For example: punches are the opposite of blocks (offense / defense), the use of the rear hand is the opposite of the use of the front hand (rear / front), and rotation from a neutral bow to a forward bow and back is a reverse (clockwise / counter clockwise).

Also, from the above break down one can quickly see that the major stance of Short Form One has to be the Neutral Bow. And, while Long Form One uses the Neutral Bow, it seems to be more preoccupied with the Forward Bow. This preoccupation with a specific stance is and will be a definite trend that is continued throughout the forms of American Kenpo. This preoccupation with a specific element of a form is referred to as a "theme" within the form. In this case, one can quickly deduce that the theme stance of Short Form One would be the Neutral Bow, while the theme stance of Long Form One would be the Forward Bow. To continue this analysis of themes, one should be able to deduce that another theme of Short Form One would be the major blocks (defense), while the theme of Long Form One would be punches (offense) and the continued expansion into non-major blocks (extending defense).

Chapter 6 - Basics of Long Form One

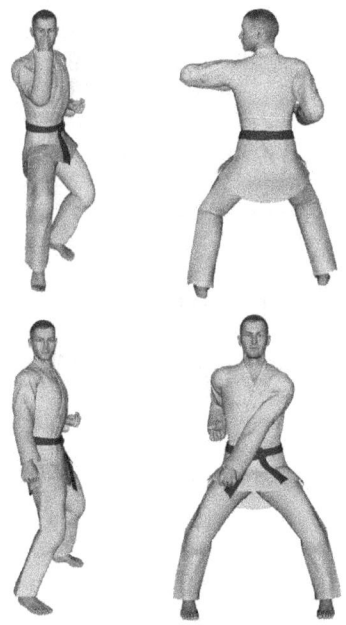

In order to properly analyze Long Form One, one must first become aware of all the basics that are employed in its execution. Since the first four forms (the one's and the two's) are considered the "dictionary" forms (i.e. they define motion), the emphasis on highlighting the basics is of greater significance than in the higher forms. In contrast, the higher forms (Short Form Three and above) tend to have more emphasis on theories and concepts over basics.

Also, by clarifying the utilized basics in Long Form One, one can begin to see how it contains and expands upon the basics of Short Form One. Glancing at the "Quick Reference of Basics" section, one can also see a high degree of uniformity and consistency throughout this form. But, this symmetry is not to the same degree as Short Form One. There are maneuvers in this form that do not have a matching counterpart (within this form). This fact opens one of the important concepts exposed in Long Form One: analysis of complimentary and categorical maneuvers and/or concepts across multiple forms. This concept shows that each form is not a self-contained entity, rather that it is a part of a whole - the American Kenpo system. And, each form has a purpose and meaning to the system.

The "Basics Utilized in Short Form One" section gives a more detailed analysis to each employed basic. This detail is provided to help in understanding the implementation and emphasis of each basic (by providing intent and method) and for remembering each step of the form (by providing direction, position, focus, and side). With this analysis, it should be fairly straightforward to re-assemble the correct execution of Long Form One.

Quick Reference of Basics

Stances:
    Meditating Horse
    Training Horse
    Fighting Horse (Upper Body / Feet) / Neutral Bow (Toe / Heel Alignment) (Left)
    Neutral Bow (Right / Left)
    Forward Bow (Upper Body) / Neutral Bow (Feet) (Left / Right)
    Forward Bow (Right / Left)
    Reverse Bow (Left)
    Cat Stance (45 degree) (Right)

Blocks (Major):
    Inward:
        Hammering (Right) (Front)
        Thrusting (Left / Right) (Front / Rear)
    Vertical Outward:
        Left / Right
        Front / Rear
    Upward:
        Left / Right
        Front / Rear
    Outside Downward (Palm Down):
        Right / Left
        Front / Rear
    Inside Downward (Palm Down):
        Left / Right
    Inside Downward (Palm Up):
        Right / Left
    Push-Down:
        Left / Right

© 2014 EPAKS Publications

Blocks (Minor):
    Inward Double Factor:
        Right / Left
        Front / Rear
    Inside Downward (Palm Up) Double Factor:
        Left / Right
        Front Rear

Strikes:
    Straight Thrust Punch:
        Left / Right
        Rear
    Upper-Cut Punch:
        Left / Right
    Outward Elbow:
        Left
        Front

Foot Maneuvers:
    Step Through (Reverse):
        Left / Right
    Step Through (Forward):
        Left
    Ninety Degree Cover:
        Right / Left
    One Hundred and Eighty Degree Cover:
        Right / Left
    Shift (with Feet) (Forward):
        Right / Left

Body Maneuver
    Shift (without Feet) (Forward / Reverse):
        Right / Left

© 2014 EPAKS Publications

Basics Utilized in Long Form One

Presented in execution order

Stances	Side	Intent	Direction	Method/Area	Focus
Meditating Horse		Major			12:00H
Neutral Bow	Right	Major	Backward (6:00H)	Step Through (Reverse)	12:00H
Forward Bow	Right	Major	Forward (12:00H)	Shift (Clockwise)	12:00H
Cat Stance 45 degree	Right	Major	Backward (6:00H)	Shift (Reverse)	12:00H
Neutral Bow	Left	Major	Backward (6:00H)	Step Through (Reverse)	12:00H
Forward Bow	Left	Major	Forward (12:00H)	Shift (Counter-Clockwise)	12:00H
Neutral Bow	Left	Major	Backward (3:00H)	90 degree Cover	9:00H
Forward Bow	Left	Major	Forward (9:00H)	Shift (Counter-Clockwise)	9:00H
Neutral Bow	Right	Major	Backward (3:00H)	Step Through (Reverse)	9:00H
Forward Bow	Right	Major	Forward (9:00H)	Shift (Clockwise)	9:00H
Reverse Bow	Left	Minor	Backward (9:00H)	180 degree Cover	3:00H
Fighting Horse (offset)	Left	Major	Forward (3:00H)	Shift (Counter-Clockwise)	3:00H
Neutral Bow	Left	Major	Forward (3:00H)	Shift (Counter-Clockwise)	3:00H
Forward Bow	Left	Major	Forward (3:00H)	Shift (Counter-Clockwise)	3:00H
Neutral Bow	Right	Major	Backward (9:00H)	Step Through (Reverse)	3:00H
Forward Bow	Right	Major	Forward (3:00H)	Shift (Clockwise)	3:00H
Neutral Bow	Right	Major	Forward (6:00H)	90 degree Cover	6:00H
Forward Bow	Right	Major	Forward (6:00H)	Shift (Clockwise)	6:00H
Neutral Bow	Left	Major	Backward (12:00H)	Step Through (Reverse)	6:00H
Forward Bow	Left	Major	Forward (6:00H)	Shift (Counter-Clockwise)	6:00H
Neutral Bow	Left	Major	Backward (12:00H)	Shift (Clockwise)	6:00H
Forward / Neutral Bow Hybrid	Left	Major	Forward (6:00H)	Shift (Counter-Clockwise)	6:00H

© 2014 EPAKS Publications

Stances	Side	Intent	Direction	Method/Area	Focus
Neutral Bow	Left	Major	Backward (12:00H)	Shift (Clockwise)	6:00H
Neutral Bow	Right	Major	Backward (12:00H)	Step Through (Reverse)	6:00H
Forward / Neutral Bow Hybrid	Right	Major	Forward (6:00H)	Shift (Clockwise)	6:00H
Neutral Bow	Right	Major	Backward (12:00H)	Shift (Counter-Clockwise)	6:00H
Neutral Bow	Right	Major	Backward (3:00H)	90 degree Cover	9:00H
Forward / Neutral Bow Hybrid	Right	Major	Forward (9:00H)	Shift (Clockwise)	9:00H
Neutral Bow	Right	Major	Backward (3:00H)	Shift (Counter-Clockwise)	9:00H
Neutral Bow	Left	Major	Backward (3:00H)	Step Through (Reverse)	9:00H
Forward / Neutral Bow Hybrid	Left	Major	Forward (9:00H)	Shift (Counter-Clockwise)	9:00H
Neutral Bow	Left	Major	Backward (3:00H)	Shift (Clockwise)	9:00H
Neutral Bow	Right	Major	Backward (9:00H)	180 degree Cover	3:00H
Forward / Neutral Bow Hybrid	Right	Major	Forward (3:00H)	Shift (Clockwise)	3:00H
Neutral Bow	Right	Major	Backward (9:00H)	Shift (Counter-Clockwise)	3:00H
Neutral Bow	Left	Major	Backward (9:00H)	Step Through (Reverse)	3:00H
Forward / Neutral Bow Hybrid	Left	Major	Forward (3:00H)	Shift (Counter-Clockwise)	3:00H
Neutral Bow	Left	Major	Backward (9:00H)	Shift (Clockwise)	3:00H
Neutral Bow	Left	Major	Backward (6:00H)	90 degree Cover	12:00H
Forward / Neutral Bow Hybrid	Left	Major	Forward (12:00H)	Shift (Counter-Clockwise)	12:00H
Neutral Bow	Left	Major	Backward (6:00H)	Shift (Clockwise)	12:00H
Neutral Bow	Right	Major	Backward (6:00H)	Step Through (Reverse)	12:00H
Forward / Neutral Bow Hybrid	Right	Major	Forward (12:00H)	Shift (Clockwise)	12:00H

© 2014 EPAKS Publications

Basics of Long Form One

Stances	Side	Intent	Direction	Method/Area	Focus
Neutral Bow	Right	Major	Backward (6:00H)	Shift (Counter-Clockwise)	12:00H
Training Horse		Major	Forward (12:00H)	Step Through (Forward)	12:00H
Meditating Horse		Major			12:00H

Blocks	Side	Intent	Direction	Position	Method/Area	Focus
Inward	Right	Major	Inward (10:30H)	Front	Hammering	12:00H
Inward	Left	Major	Inward (1:30H)	Front	Thrusting	12:00H
Inward	Right	Minor	Inward (7:30H)	Rear	Thrusting	9:00H
Vertical Outward	Left	Major	Outward (6:00H)	Front	Thrusting	9:00H
Inward	Left	Minor	Inward (10:30H)	Rear	Hammering	9:00H
Vertical Outward	Right	Major	Outward (9:00H)	Front	Thrusting	9:00H
Upward	Left	Major	Upward (12:00V / 3:00H)	Front	Thrusting	3:00H
Inward	Left	Minor	Inward (4:30H)	Rear	Hammering	3:00H
Upward	Right	Major	Upward (12:00V / 3:00H)	Front	Thrusting	3:00H
Inside Downward (Palm Up)	Left	Minor	Inward (9:00H) / Downward (6:00V)	Rear	Thrusting	6:00H
Outside Downward (Palm Down)	Right	Major	Downward (6:00V) / Outward (9:00H)	Front	Hammering	6:00H
Inside Downward (Palm Up)	Right	Minor	Inward (3:00H) / Downward (6:00V)	Rear	Thrusting	6:00H
Outside Downward (Palm Down)	Left	Major	Downward (6:00V) / Outward (3:00H)	Front	Hammering	6:00H
Inward	Left	Major	Inward (7:30H)	Front	Thrusting	6:00H
Inward	Right	Major	Inward (4:30H)	Rear	Thrusting	6:00H
Inward	Left	Major	Inward (7:30H)	Front	Thrusting	6:00H
Inward	Right	Major	Inward (4:30H)	Front	Thrusting	6:00H
Inward	Left	Major	Inward (7:30H)	Rear	Thrusting	6:00H
Inward	Right	Major	Inward (4:30H)	Front	Thrusting	6:00H
Inward	Left	Minor	Inward (10:30H)	Rear	Thrusting	9:00H
Vertical Outward	Right	Major	Outward (12:00H)	Front	Thrusting	9:00H
Inward	Right	Minor	Inward (7:30H)	Front	Thrusting	9:00H
Vertical Outward	Left	Major	Outward (6:00H)	Rear	Thrusting	9:00H
Inward	Left	Minor	Inward (10:30H)	Rear	Thrusting	9:00H
Vertical Outward	Right	Major	Outward (12:00H)	Front	Thrusting	9:00H

© 2014 EPAKS Publications

The Official EPAKS Guide to Long Form One

Blocks	Side	Intent	Direction	Position	Method/Area	Focus
Inward	Right	Minor	Inward (7:30H)	Front	Thrusting	9:00H
Vertical Outward	Left	Major	Outward (6:00H)	Front	Thrusting	9:00H
Inward	Left	Minor	Inward (10:30H)	Front	Thrusting	9:00H
Vertical Outward	Right	Major	Outward (12:00H)	Rear	Thrusting	9:00H
Inward	Right	Minor	Inward (7:30H)	Rear	Thrusting	9:00H
Vertical Outward	Left	Major	Outward (6:00H)	Front	Thrusting	9:00H
Inward	Left	Minor	Inward (4:30H)	Rear	Thrusting	3:00H
Upward	Right	Major	Upward (12:00V / 3:00H)	Front	Thrusting	3:00H
Inward	Right	Minor	Inward (1:30H)	Front	Hammering	3:00H
Upward	Left	Major	Upward (12:00V / 3:00H)	Rear	Thrusting	3:00H
Inward	Left	Minor	Inward (4:30H)	Rear	Hammering	3:00H
Upward	Right	Major	Upward (12:00V / 3:00H)	Front	Thrusting	3:00H
Inward	Right	Minor	Inward (1:30H)	Front	Hammering	3:00H
Upward	Left	Major	Upward (12:00V / 3:00H)	Front	Thrusting	3:00H
Inward	Left	Minor	Inward (4:30H)	Front	Thrusting	3:00H
Upward	Right	Major	Upward (12:00V / 3:00H)	Rear	Thrusting	3:00H
Inward	Right	Minor	Inward (1:30H)	Rear	Hammering	3:00H
Upward	Left	Major	Upward (12:00V / 3:00H)	Front	Thrusting	3:00H
Inside Downward (Palm Up)	Right	Minor	Inward (9:00H) / Downward (6:00V)	Rear	Hammering	12:00H
Outside Downward (Palm Down)	Left	Major	Downward (6:00V) / Outward (9:00H)	Front	Hammering	12:00H
Inside Downward (Palm Up)	Left	Minor	Inward (3:00H) / Downward (6:00V)	Front	Hammering	12:00H
Outside Downward (Palm Down)	Right	Major	Downward (6:00V) / Outward (3:00H)	Rear	Hammering	12:00H
Inside Downward (Palm Up)	Right	Minor	Inward (9:00H) / Downward (6:00V)	Rear	Hammering	12:00H
Outside Downward (Palm Down)	Left	Major	Downward (6:00V) / Outward (9:00H)	Front	Hammering	12:00H
Inside Downward (Palm Up)	Left	Minor	Inward (3:00H) / Downward (6:00V)	Front	Hammering	12:00H

© 2014 EPAKS Publications

Basics of Long Form One

Blocks	Side	Intent	Direction	Position	Method/Area	Focus
Outside Downward (Palm Down)	Right	Major	Downward (6:00V) / Outward (3:00H)	Front	Hammering	12:00H
Inside Downward (Palm Up)	Right	Minor	Inward (3:00H) / Downward (6:00V)	Front	Hammering	12:00H
Outside Downward (Palm Down)	Left	Major	Downward (6:00V) / Outward (9:00H)	Rear	Hammering	12:00H
Inside Downward (Palm Up)	Left	Minor	Inward (3:00H) / Downward (6:00V)	Front	Hammering	12:00H
Outside Downward (Palm Down)	Right	Major	Downward (6:00V) / Outward (3:00H)	Front	Hammering	12:00H
Inside Downward (Palm Down)	Left	Major	Downward (6:00V) / Inward (3:00H)		Thrusting	12:00H
Inside Downward (Palm Down)	Right	Major	Downward (6:00V) / Inward (9:00H)		Thrusting	12:00H
Inside Downward (Palm Down)	Left	Major	Downward (6:00V) / Inward (3:00H)		Thrusting	12:00H
Inside Downward (Palm Up)	Right	Major	Downward (6:00V) / Inward (9:00H)		Hammering	12:00H
Inside Downward (Palm Up)	Left	Major	Downward (6:00V) / Inward (3:00H)		Hammering	12:00H
Inside Downward (Palm Up)	Right	Major	Downward (6:00V) / Inward (9:00H)		Hammering	12:00H
Push Down	Left	Major	Downward (6:00V)		Pressing	12:00H
Push Down	Right	Major	Downward (6:00V)		Pressing	12:00H
Push Down	Left	Major	Downward (6:00V)		Pressing	12:00H

Strikes	Side	Intent	Direction	Position	Method/Area	Focus
Straight Punch	Left	Major	Forward (12:00H)	Rear	Thrusting	12:00H
Straight Punch	Right	Major	Forward (12:00H)	Rear	Thrusting	12:00H
Straight Punch	Right	Major	Forward (9:00H)	Rear	Thrusting	9:00H
Straight Punch	Left	Major	Forward (9:00H)	Rear	Thrusting	9:00H

© 2014 EPAKS Publications

Strikes	Side	Intent	Direction	Position	Method/Area	Focus
Horizontal Outward Elbow	Left	Major	Outward (3:00H)	Front	Thrusting	3:00H
Straight Punch	Right	Major	Forward (3:00H)	Rear	Thrusting	3:00H
Straight Punch	Left	Major	Forward (3:00H)	Rear	Thrusting	3:00H
Straight Punch	Left	Major	Forward (6:00H)	Rear	Thrusting	6:00H
Straight Punch	Right	Major	Forward (6:00H)	Rear	Thrusting	6:00H
Straight Punch	Right	Major	Forward (12:00H)		Thrusting	12:00H
Straight Punch	Left	Major	Forward (12:00H)		Thrusting	12:00H
Straight Punch	Right	Major	Forward Diagonal (10:30H)		Thrusting	12:00H
Straight Punch	Left	Major	Forward Diagonal (1:30H)		Thrusting	12:00H
Straight Punch	Right	Major	Inward (9:00H)		Thrusting	12:00H
Straight Punch	Left	Major	Inward (3:00H)		Thrusting	12:00H
Uppercut Punch	Right	Major	Upward Diagonal (12:00V) / 12:00H)		Thrusting	12:00H
Uppercut Punch	Left	Major	Upward Diagonal (12:00V) / 12:00H)		Thrusting	12:00H

Foot & Body Maneuvers	Side	Intent	Direction	Focus
Step Through	Left	Major	Backward (6:00H)	12:00H
Shift (Rotation)	Right	Major	Forward (12:00H)	12:00H
Shift (Distance)	Right	Major	Backward (6:00H)	12:00H
Step Through	Right	Major	Backward (6:00H)	12:00H
Shift (Rotation)	Left	Major	Forward (12:00H)	12:00H
90 degree Cover	Right	Major	Backward (3:00H)	9:00H
Shift (Rotation)	Left	Major	Forward (9:00H)	9:00H
Step Through	Left	Major	Backward (3:00H)	9:00H
Shift	Right	Major	Forward (9:00H)	9:00H
180 degree Cover	Right	Major	Backward (9:00H)	3:00H
Shift (Rotation)	Left	Major	Forward (3:00H)	3:00H
Shift (Rotation)	Left	Major	Forward (3:00H)	3:00H
Shift (Rotation)	Left	Major	Forward (3:00H)	3:00H
Step Through	Left	Major	Backward (9:00H)	3:00H
Shift (Rotation)	Right	Major	Forward (3:00H)	3:00H
90 degree Cover	Right	Major	Forward (6:00H)	6:00H
Shift	Right	Major	Forward (6:00H)	6:00H
Step Through	Right	Major	Backward (12:00H)	6:00H
Shift	Left	Major	Forward (6:00H)	6:00H

© 2014 EPAKS Publications

Basics of Long Form One — 175

Foot & Body Maneuvers	Side	Intent	Direction	Focus
Shift	Right	Major	Backward (12:00H)	6:00H
Rotation (without Shift)	Left	Major	Forward (6:00H)	6:00H
Rotation (without Shift)	Right	Major	Backward (12:00H)	6:00H
Step Through	Left	Major	Backward (12:00H)	6:00H
Rotation (without Shift)	Right	Major	Forward (6:00H)	6:00H
Rotation (without Shift)	Left	Major	Backward (12:00H)	6:00H
90 degree Cover	Left	Major	Backward (3:00H)	9:00H
Rotation (without Shift)	Right	Major	Forward (9:00H)	9:00H
Rotation (without Shift)	Left	Major	Backward (3:00H)	9:00H
Step Through	Right	Major	Backward (3:00H)	9:00H
Rotation (without Shift)	Left	Major	Forward (9:00H)	9:00H
Rotation (without Shift)	Right	Major	Backward (3:00H)	9:00H
180 degree Cover	Left	Major	Backward (3:00H)	3:00H
Rotation (without Shift)	Right	Major	Forward (3:00H)	3:00H
Rotation (without Shift)	Left	Major	Backward (9:00H)	3:00H
Step Through	Right	Major	Backward (9:00H)	3:00H
Rotation (without Shift)	Left	Major	Forward (3:00H)	3:00H
Rotation (without Shift)	Right	Major	Backward (9:00H)	3:00H
90 degree Cover	Right	Major	Backward (6:00H)	12:00H
Rotation (without Shift)	Left	Major	Forward (12:00H)	12:00H
Rotation (without Shift)	Right	Major	Backward (6:00H)	12:00H
Step Through	Left	Major	Backward (6:00H)	12:00H
Rotation (without Shift)	Right	Major	Forward (12:00H)	12:00H
Rotation (without Shift)	Left	Major	Backward (6:00H)	12:00H
Step Through (1/2)	Left	Major	Forward (12:00H)	12:00H

© 2014 EPAKS Publications

Chapter 7 - Analysis of Long Form One

In order to analyze Long Form One, One must first answer two simple questions:

1) What is it that is being analyzed?
2) What is the purpose of the analysis?

Analysis of Long Form One | 177

What is being analyzed?

The obvious answer is Long Form One is being analyzed. But what is Long Form One? In the most fundamental terms, Long Form One is a series of basics executed together to create a form. But, what is the purpose of creating a form? As mentioned earlier in this guide, American Kenpo forms are not to be thought of as a choreographed fight between the practitioner and (an) imaginary opponent(s) for demonstration purposes. American Kenpo forms are defined as:

> A predefined series of maneuvers that:
> 1) show the rules and principles of motion,
> 2) that everything has a reverse and an opposite,
> 3) by giving an example

Provided with the above information, one can move on to the second question posed.

What is the purpose of the analysis?

Again, the obvious answer is to expose the information presented in Long Form One. But, what information is being exposed? From the definition derived above, one can limit their analysis to the three elements that compose the definition. Then, the major question that should now be asked is, "how will the exposed information be presented?"

The information exposed from Long Form One will be broken down into four sections:

© 2014 EPAKS Publications

Beginner / Intermediate Analysis
This section will discuss and summarize the information for which a beginner to intermediate practitioner should be aware. This is important because not all readers are advanced practitioners. This section will help them check what they know against what should be known about Long Form One – at the beginner to intermediate level. Also, this section is helpful to instructors, for it will help them filter what information should be conveyed when initially teaching this form to others.

Advanced Analysis
This section will discuss and summarize the information for which an advanced practitioner should be aware. It is intended for the advanced practitioners and instructors. It covers some of the lesser known information related to Long Form One.

Reverse / Opposite Analysis
This section will collate and expose the reverse / opposite information presented in the form. This is important because, by definition, American Kenpo forms give an example of reverses and opposites. This section is intended to help simplify this analysis by exposing the reverses and opposites for each section of the form.

Principles / Rules / Theories / Concepts / Definitions
This section will list the terms related to Long Form One. Each term will need to be further researched by the reader. This section is provided mainly as a starting point into further analysis of American Kenpo terminology, concepts, theories, rules, and principles.

Intra vs Inter Form Analysis

When analyzing any form, one must first consider the scope of their analysis. Does the analysis only include the form itself, or does the analysis include other forms in the system? Any analysis should first start with the form itself, and then expand to include the rest of the forms in the system.

In other words, each form can be thought of as both a self-contained entity, and a component of a larger structure. By thinking of the forms in this way, one can build boundaries in which to perform their analysis. Analysis contained within the boundaries of the form is referred to as intra-form analysis. Analysis outside of the boundaries of the form is referred to as inter-form analysis.

One suggested way in which to progress through the analysis of a form is to begin by examining each element of the form, comparing and contrasting it to other elements of the form, to ultimately build up an analysis of the entire form. The next step would be to expand the analysis to the earlier forms, looking to find ways in which the current form completes missing information, while also adding to the knowledge base of the lower forms. Next, as new forms are learned, this method of analysis should repeat itself with this newly learned form. And for the final step, the practitioner should go back to each of the previously known forms, filling in any newly discovered pieces of information that were previously overlooked or not known until exposed by the learning of the new form.

In the case of Long Form One, inter-form analysis is easier than in higher forms. This is mainly due to the fact that Long Form One, in essence, contains the entirety of Short Form One. The main difference being that the Short Form One section is executed on the left side. This is not the case in the higher forms. Therefore, as analysis of the forms progresses, inter-form analysis becomes more complex.

Beginning / Intermediate Analysis

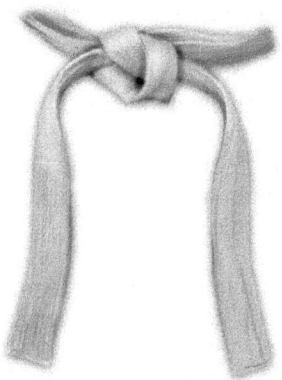

This section will cover the analysis of Long Form One from the perspective of what should be known, learned and / or taught to the novice to intermediate practitioner. One would be justified in asking why not just analyze Long Form One in one overarching section? Why segment out the analysis into two major sections - Beginner / Intermediate and Advanced? There are a number of reasons for this format.

First, by splitting the analysis in this way, a beginning to intermediate reader can be exposed to just information for which they should be aware; without being mired down in information that is way beyond their current knowledge level of the American Kenpo system. Secondly, from an instructor's perspective by splitting the analysis in this manner this guide book can be used to summarize the information that an instructor should be imparting to their students about Long Form One.

Also, since the American Kenpo system is composed of many principles, rules, theories, concepts, ideas, definitions, and maneuvers, it is very easy for the beginning to intermediate practitioner to be overwhelmed with information about a seemingly easy form. By segmenting the information, it makes exposure to the comprehensive knowledge base of the American Kenpo system less intimidating and overwhelming. This methodology is also applicable to the instructor as they teach the information about Long Form One to their student(s). Too much information in a short period of time can sometimes be just as bad as too little.

Finally, the information in this section tends to be information that is commonly presented. In other words, information in this section is more openly taught by instructors about Long Form One. The information in the Advanced Analysis section tends more towards self-exposed information - that is, information that the practitioner them-self should be able to deduce on their own, with little to no help from an instructor. That being said, this section is a building block for the Advanced Analysis section. By using the method of analysis presented in this section, much of the information presented in the Advanced Analysis section should be deducible through self-analysis of Long Form One on one's own.

As a final note: It is advisable that the beginner to intermediate practitioner review the information presented in this section numerous times. By doing this, the reader will be able to reflect on and get comfortable with any new information learned from this section. Then, at a future date, come back to this same section, review the reflected upon information, and hopefully glean more new information through each repeated exposure to this section - until all of the information presented in this section is easily recalled and understood.

Walk-Through Analysis

As stated numerous times throughout this guide, Long Form One is designed to start with the information presented in Short Form One and build upon it. One way to illustrate how the information is compounded is to step through both forms and explain the information exposed from each maneuver. Through this approach the reader will be presented with the obvious information, but also the not so obvious information will be revealed. Or to put it another way: the user will be confronted with the information hidden in plain sight. Information that is demonstrated, but not necessarily explained. Or if explained, not explained thoroughly.

In Short Form One the first maneuver is as follows: step back into a right neutral bow while delivering a hammering, right, inward block to the front. The obvious information derived from this maneuver is:
- the maneuver retreats
- the block is defensive
- the block is executed with the front arm
- the block is executed with the right arm

- the block is delivered using the power principle of torque
- the stance utilized is the right neutral bow

In Long Form One the first maneuver is executed exactly the same as in Short Form One. And, contains the exact same information.

The second maneuver is as follows: shift forward into a right forward bow while delivering a thrusting, left, straight punch to the front. The obvious information derived from this maneuver is:
- the punch is offensive
- the punch is executed using the rear arm
- the punch is executed using the power principle of torque
- the punch is executed by shifting into a forward bow

Analyzing this information further - the punch exposes the following new information:
- offense is the opposite of defense
- the rear (arm) is the opposite of the front (arm)
- the punch rotation is in the reverse direction of the block rotation
- the forward bow is a new stance with a set of new properties

---

The next maneuver is as follows: draw the right foot backward towards the left into a right 45 degree cat stance while simultaneously raising the right arm to a vertical, covering position to the front. The obvious information derived from this maneuver is:
- although this position is transitory at other points in the form, it is highlighted here
- this maneuver is not explicitly executed in Short Form One
- the 45 degree cat stance is a new stance

© 2014 EPAKS Publications

Analysis of Long Form One   185

- the raising of the front arm is not used for defense

Analyzing this information further exposes the following new information:
- the covering block exposes the intersection position of the blocks
- the cat stance exposes the intersection position of the stances
- this maneuver previews new information (intersections) that will be expanded upon in the next form
- the cat stance forces the practitioner to shift their weight onto the rear leg preventing them from shifting their left heel prior to executing the step through (Economy of Motion) - which is a common execution error

---

The next few (six) maneuvers reiterate information presented above - but also include information for the opposite (left) side.

The next maneuvers that need to be analyzed are the steps prior to the first upward block sequence: right, 180 degree, cover step and execution of the left outward elbow, followed by the dropping of the left arm prior to executing the left upward block. The obvious information derived from these maneuvers is:
- the elbow is a short range, offensive weapon (contrasted to the long range punch)
- the elbow is not executed to the front (like the punches)
- the elbow is executed while shifting into a horse (not a forward bow)
- the elbow is executed with the front arm (not the rear)
- the fighting horse is a new stance
- the dropping of the elbow is to gain Path of Travel for the upward block (to make it more effective)

Analyzing this information further exposes the following new information:

© 2014 EPAKS Publications

- execution of a maneuver doesn't always have to be toward the front
- execution of an offensive maneuver doesn't always have to be while shifting into a forward bow (like the punches)
- execution of an offensive maneuver can be done with the front arm (opposite)
- exposure to new concepts including: Path of Travel and Pivot Point

---

The next few (three) maneuvers continue to reiterate information presented previously.

The next maneuver that needs to be analyzed is the first downward block: right, 90 degree, cover step forward with a right downward block. The obvious information derived from this maneuver is:
- the step is forward

Analyzing this information further exposes the following new information:
- execution of a defensive maneuver doesn't always have to be done while retreating
- this maneuver previews what will be expanded upon (advancing) in the Two's
- this maneuver is done in the reverse direction of all of the previous maneuvers (advancing)

The next few (three) maneuvers continue to reiterate information presented previously.

Analysis of Long Form One   187

The whole next section of the form can be analyzed as a single entity since it is the same information repeated for each of the blocks: block three times for each of the blocks, alternating between the front and rear arm for the Inward, Vertical Outward, Upward, and Outside Downward blocks. The obvious information derived from these maneuvers is:
- this entire section is the repeat of Short Form One, only executed with both the front and rear arms

Analyzing this information further exposes the following new information:
- this entire section is the left side of Short Form One
- this entire section is done facing the opposite direction of Short Form One
- a defense does not have to be executed from only the front arm

---

The next maneuvers that need to be analyzed are the inside-downward, palm down blocks of the isolation. The obvious information derived from these maneuvers is:
- these blocks are new types of blocks
- these blocks are executed for both the left and right side
- these blocks are executed without any rotation of stance
- these blocks are executed with a thrusting Method of Execution

Analyzing this information further exposes the following new information:
- these blocks are executed on the reverse line of the downward blocks

---

The next maneuvers that need to be analyzed are the inside-downward, palm up blocks of the isolation. The obvious information derived from these maneuvers is:
- these blocks are new types of blocks
- these blocks are executed for both the left and right side

© 2014 EPAKS Publications

- these blocks are executed without any rotation of stance
- these blocks are executed with a hammering Method of Execution

Analyzing this information further exposes the following new information:
- these blocks are executed on the reverse line of the downward blocks
- these blocks are executed with the palm facing in the opposite direction of the palm-down blocks

---

The next maneuvers that need to be analyzed are the push-down blocks of the isolation. The obvious information derived from these maneuvers is:
- these blocks are new types of blocks
- these blocks are executed for both the left and right side
- these blocks are executed without any rotation of stance
- these blocks are executed with the hand open

Analyzing this information further exposes the following new information:
- these blocks are executed on the opposite line of the downward blocks - i.e. vertical
- these blocks are executed on the reverse line of the upward blocks - i.e. vertically downward
- these blocks are executed using the palm of the hand as the Point of Contact - rather than the forearm

---

The next maneuvers that need to be analyzed are the straight punches toward 12:00H of the isolation. The obvious information derived from these maneuvers is:
- these punches are executed like the previous punches - only from a horse stance
- these punches are executed for both the left and right side

Analysis of Long Form One 189

Analyzing this information further exposes the following new information:
- these punches are executed without a shift in stance
- these punches start a pattern that is continued throughout the entire punch sequence of the isolation

---

The next maneuvers that need to be analyzed are the straight punches toward 10:30H & 1:30H of the isolation. The obvious information derived from these maneuvers is:
- these punches are executed to a new line - diagonal
- these punches are executed for both the left and right side

Analyzing this information further exposes the following new information:
- these punches are executed without a shift in stance
- these punches preview the new line(s) that will be used during the execution of the Two's (Short and Long)

The next maneuvers that need to be analyzed are the straight punches toward 9:00H - 3:00H of the isolation. The obvious information derived from these maneuvers is:
- these punches are executed on straight lines to the side
- these punches are executed for both the left and right side

Analyzing this information further exposes the following new information:
- these punches are executed without a shift in stance

The next maneuvers that need to be analyzed are the uppercut punches toward 12:00H of the isolation. The obvious information derived from these maneuvers is:
- these punches are new types of punches

© 2014 EPAKS Publications

- these punches are executed for both the left and right side

Analyzing this information further exposes the following new information:
- these punches are executed on the opposite line of the other punches - i.e. upward (vertical)
- these punches are executed with the palm facing in the opposite direction of the other punches

Analysis of Long Form One 191

Summary

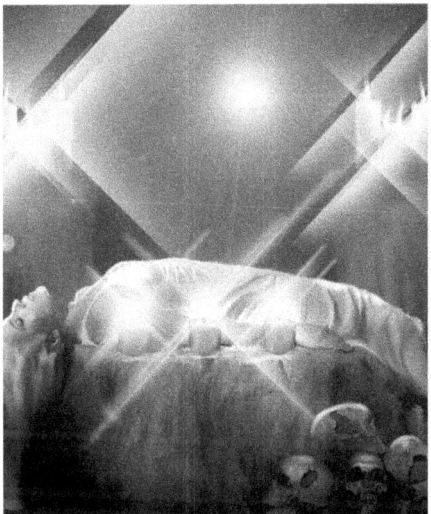

Long Form One introduces:

1)
The concept of a Long form. This sets the concepts that the practitioner must learn:
  a) Long forms include the information presented in the Short form
  b) Long forms extend the information presented in the Short form

2)
The following new stances:
  a) Forward Bow - which introduces the following new concepts:
    i) Brace Angle
    ii) Weight Distribution (60% / 40%)
    iii) close distance without foot maneuver
  b) 45 degree Cat - which introduces the following new concepts:
    i) Intersection Position
    ii) Positional Cover

© 2014 EPAKS Publications

iii) Weight Distribution (10% / 90%)
c) Reverse Bow - which introduces the following new concepts:
   i) Weight Distribution (40% / 60%)
   ii) create distance without foot maneuver
d) Horse - which introduces the following new concepts:
   i) Isolation

3) The concept of offense. This sets the concepts that the practitioner must learn:
   a) the definition of strike:
      i) any offensive maneuver executed with the intention of causing injury to the opponent
   b) each strike has a proper height, depth, and width of execution
   c) strikes should make contact with the target at a proper depth of range (aka Point of Focus)
   d) strikes should be executed utilizing:
      i) Body Alignment
      ii) Body Fusion
      iii) Angle of Incidence
      iv) Focus Point

4) The following new strikes:
   a) straight thrusting punch - which introduces the following:
      i) the definition of a punch:
         A) a specialized strike which utilizes the front of the first two knuckles of the fist as it's Point of Contact
      ii) Contouring - of self (during delivery)
      iii) Strike ranges:
         A) short range
         B) medium range
         C) long range
      iv) striking to a new range - long range
   b) back elbow - which introduces the following:
      i) Striking to a new range - short range

Analysis of Long Form One

c) uppercut punch - which introduces the following:
  i) striking in a upward direction (vertical)
  iii) punching to a new range - short range

5) The following new blocks:
  a) inward block (with the rear arm)
  b) outward block (with the rear arm)
  c) upward block (with the rear arm)
  d) downward block (with the rear arm)
  e) inside-downward block - palm down
  f) inside-downward block - palm up
  g) push-down block - which introduces the following:
    i) defense against a strike coming from an upward (vertical) angle of attack

6) The concept of shifting from a Neutral Bow to a Forward bow. This sets the concepts that the practitioner must learn:
  a) Body Rotation to generate power
  b) Opposing Forces to aid in generating power (retraction of opposite arm)
  c) Back-Up Mass as a minor power principle
  d) shifting of weight with strike to aid in generating power
  e) Brace Angle to aid in supporting strike
  f) Body Alignment to aid in generating power and supporting strike

7) Transitional maneuvers:
  a) Cat (during step-through) - which introduces the following:
    i) Stepping-through without 'breaking the heel' of your rear foot
  b) Covering - which introduces the following:
    i) Covers are composed of the following elements:
      A) distance (change)
      B) rotation (into new stance)
    ii) Covers can be used to:

A) create distance
B) close distance

8) The concept of shifting from a Neutral Bow to a specialized Forward bow. This sets the concepts that the practitioner must learn:
   a) upper Body Rotation disconnected from lower body rotation
   b) increase of rear hand reach without change in lower body

9) The concept of shifting from a Reverse Bow to a specialized Horse. This sets the concepts that the practitioner must learn:
   a) changing a rear hand strike to the front hand through the use of a cover step and shifting Point of Reference

10) The concept of stepping forward with a cover step. This sets the concepts that the practitioner must learn:
    a) close distance with a foot maneuver
    b) reverse line of defense

11) The concept of Isolation maneuvers. This sets the concepts that the practitioner must learn:
    a) upper body maneuvers can be executed from a stationary position
    b) that isolation maneuvers show:
       i) previews of things to come
       ii) new information
       iii) missing information

Long Form One falls into the category of a dictionary form. As such, it continues the following elements of the dictionary forms.

Analysis of Long Form One

1) The blocking sequence:
    a) In
    b) Out
    c) Up
    d) Down

2) The form starts from the meditating horse stance.

Long Form One has a number of other elements it teaches:

1) It is defined as follows:
    a) it is a front hand and rear hand defense form
    b) it is a rear / front hand offense form
    c) it is an advancing with defense only form
    d) major offense only form
    e) it is the extension to Short Form One

2) The opposite hand should be chambered in-sync with the striking hand. The reverse motion of the retracting arm then emphasizes and optimizes the power generated by the front arm.

3) Single beat timing (i.e. one in one timing)

4) Defense then offense with opposite hands

5) Basic timing for both defensive and offensive maneuvers

6) The use of double factor moves while advancing

7)
    The use of both upper case and lower case maneuvers

Advanced Analysis

This section will cover the analysis of Long Form One from an advanced perspective. Before continuing forward into this section, it is advised that the reader be very comfortable with the majority of information presented in the Beginning / Intermediate Analysis section and its methodology of analysis. It is the purpose of this section to expose the reader to information that is usually not openly presented by an instructor until later in a practitioner's training, or eluded to at some point during a review of the form with an instructor, or not at all. One may ask - why not at all? To be perfectly frank, some of the information contained in the forms was designed by SGM Parker to be self-exposed information. That is: information the practitioner was expected to deduce for themself after being taught how to analyze the motion contained in American Kenpo forms - i.e. after the information and methodology of analysis presented in the Beginner / Intermediate Analysis section became common knowledge. The scenario for how this succession of information was supposed to work is as follows:

The instructor was to teach form 'x' to the student. This consisted of all the maneuvers along with some information about the maneuvers and how they generally fit into the American Kenpo system. Then, through repeated review, the instructor was to expose more information and also allude to the fact that their was still yet more information which needed to be uncovered by the student. At which point the student was then instructed to reflect further upon the form and ask questions to the instructor (and possibly other students) about the information deduced through this self-analysis. Through this process it was intended that the instructor guide the student into self-exposing more and more information about the form - until all the information was exposed. And, ultimately the student became self-dependent - and completely able to think and deduce information on their own.

One may then further ask - if this is supposed to be mainly self-exposed information, why is this type of information illustrated in this section? Again to be perfectly frank, the above scenario didn't completely work as intended - for numerous reasons. Most of which are self-evident to any serious, long term practitioner of American Kenpo. In the end, the final result was that, in general, less and less information was passed down to each generation further from SGM Parker. And, to make matters worse, the practitioners were not even aware of the fact that there was more information contained in the forms than what they were exposed to by their instructor. Therefore, this section can be used by instructors and advanced practitioners to reclaim, re-acquaint, refresh, and / or learn the 'lost' or 'hidden' information contained in the form.

As recommended in the Beginning / Intermediate Analysis section, the information presented in this section should be examined through numerous passes over a long period of time. Through this practice, the reader will often uncover new, overlooked information that was not readily apparent from a previous review. And, through repeated exposure and contemplation, the information presented will become easier and easier to absorb, while simultaneously improving self-discovery of information contained in the form.

Walk-Through Analysis

As stated numerous times throughout this guide, Long Form One is designed to start with the information presented in Short Form One and build upon it. One way to illustrate how the information is compounded is to step through both forms and explain the information exposed from each maneuver. Through this approach the reader will not only be exposed to some of the less known information presented in both forms but more importantly be exposed to constructing a thought pattern for comparing and contrasting information presented throughout the American Kenpo system. The importance of using this thought pattern for advanced analysis cannot be over emphasized. By analyzing American Kenpo through this specific methodology, one can begin to learn how to think properly about the composition of information contained therein and ultimately learn to self-expose more aspects of the design of American Kenpo, beyond what is presented in this guide. Or as SGM Parker put it: "learn to think for yourself."

In order to fully appreciate the analysis being utilized below, one must first analyze the analysis itself. First, the analysis looks at opposites of motion, then reverses of motion, and then new information. Next, the analysis looks into the concepts of the motion - uncovering any opposites, reverses, or new concepts.

In Long Form One the first maneuver is as follows: step back into a right neutral bow while delivering a hammering, right, inward block to the front. An analysis of this maneuver exposes the following information:
- the maneuver is executed with one-in-one timing
- the block is delivered with the side of the weapon (arm)
- the block is executed with right arm first - i.e. the strong side
- the Method of Execution of the block is hammering due to the Point of Origin of the arm during the salutation
- the retraction of the rear arm to a chambered position places the practitioner in a "non-realistic' position - i.e. the rear hand is not checking
- the retraction of the rear arm to a chambered position places the rear hand out of the Line of Sight for the next maneuver
- the concept of - Path of Travel

In Long Form One the first maneuver is executed exactly the same as in Short Form One. And, contains the exact same information.

The second maneuver is as follows: shift forward into a right forward bow while delivering a thrusting, left, straight punch to the front. An analysis of this maneuver exposes the following information:
- the punch is delivered with the tip of the arm - instead of the side of the arm
- the punch is executed linearly
- the shift forward causes the practitioner to slightly Close the Gap

Analysis of Long Form One

- the punch also employs the power principle of back-up mass
- the punch introduces new concepts - Line of Travel
- the opposite arm is retracted creating an unchecked posture
- the forward bow introduces new concepts - Brace Angle
- the forward bow dramatically increases the range of the rear arm

---

The next maneuver is as follows: draw the right foot backward towards the left into a right 45 degree cat stance while simultaneously raising the right arm to a vertical, covering position to the front. An analysis of this maneuver exposes the following information:
- the principle of - Economy of Motion (for the step through reverse foot maneuver)
- the concept of - "almost anything you can do with your upper body, you can do with your lower body"
- the concept of - Breaking the Heel

The next few (six) maneuvers reiterate information presented above - but also include information for the opposite (left) side.

The next maneuvers that need to be analyzed are the steps prior to the first upward block sequence: right, 180 degree, cover step and execution of the left outward elbow, followed by the dropping of the left arm prior to executing the left upward block. An analysis of these maneuvers exposes the following information:
- the rotation to the horse from a reverse bow exposes the reverse rotation that is utilized for the punches
- the step exposes the reverse forward bow stance (prior to the rotation)
- the cover step is broken into multiple steps exposing its component pieces (distance and rotation)

© 2014 EPAKS Publications

- the cover step exposes how to change a rear weapon into a front weapon by changing the Point of Reference
- the cover step exposes a hybrid horse / neutral bow stance (offset horse)
- the elbow exposes an offensive weapon with the opposite end (tip) of the weapon (from the punch)
- the elbow exposes new concepts including: Compact Unit, Close Range, Degree of Rotation, etc.
- the elbow highlights the concept: Line of Travel and Reverse Motion
- the anchoring of the elbow exposes using the fist as a pivot point (instead of the shoulder / elbow)
- the anchoring of the elbow exposes a new way of maneuvering the arm into the intersection position
- the anchoring of the elbow eliminates the need for a double factor

---

The next few (three) maneuvers continue to reiterate information presented previously.

The next maneuver that needs to be analyzed is the first downward block: right, 90 degree, cover step forward with a right downward block. An analysis of this maneuver exposes the following information:
- the concept - Close the Gap
- the step forward is the reverse of the step backward

The next few (three) maneuvers continue to reiterate information presented previously.

© 2014 EPAKS Publications

Analysis of Long Form One

The whole next section of the form can be analyzed as a single entity since it is the same information repeated for each of the blocks: block three times for each of the blocks, alternating between the front and rear arm for the Inward, Vertical Outward, Upward, and Outside Downward blocks. An analysis of these maneuvers exposes the following information:
- this entire section adds missing direct / counter - rotational information to Short Form One
- the concept - Degree of Rotation (as applied to stances)
- the isolation of the lower body from the upper body exposes a hybrid neural / forward bow stance
- the concept of - Partial extended range of the rear arm (contrasted with the forward bow)

The next maneuvers that need to be analyzed are the inside-downward, palm down blocks of the isolation. An analysis of these maneuvers exposes the following information:
- the first block is not part of the isolation (because it is executed with the cover step forward) - because of this, it is mandated that the blocks are executed in groups of three (3), while the punches are executed in groups of two (2)
- these blocks expose cocking to the downward (natural) position

---

The next maneuvers that need to be analyzed are the inside-downward, palm up blocks of the isolation. An analysis of these maneuvers exposes the following information:
- these blocks are executed with a restricted Path of Travel (to center-line)
- these block expose cocking to the upward position

It should be noted that this time that the isolation does not show the outside-downward, palm up blocks. They are purposefully omitted.

The next maneuvers that need to be analyzed are the push-down blocks of the isolation. An analysis of these maneuvers exposes the following information:
- these blocks are intended to stop an on-coming attack - not create an Angle of Deflection
- these blocks display Close Range defense
- this is the first time that any maneuver is executed in the forms with an open hand
- highlight the concept of - Margin for Error

The next maneuvers that need to be analyzed are the straight punches toward 12:00H, 10:30H & 1:30H, and 9:00H - 3:00H of the isolation. An analysis of these maneuvers exposes the following information:
- these punches demonstrate the 5 major linear angles to which punches can be effectively executed on the horizontal plane
- the (9:00H - 3:00H) punches do not obey the concept of Body Alignment

The next maneuvers that need to be analyzed are the uppercut punches toward 12:00H of the isolation. An analysis of these maneuvers exposes the following information:
- these punches display Close Range offense

Analysis of Long Form One

Summary

Long Form One introduces:

1)
    Each of the concepts introduced in the short form are applicable to this form

2)
    The concept that each form has a predominant (or theme) stance. In this case, the Forward Bow.

3)
    The following new strikes:
    a) straight thrusting punch - which introduces the following:
        i) directions from which a punch can be effectively executed:
            A) 12:00
            B) 10:30
            C) 1:30
            D) 9:00
            E) 3:00

ii) Line of Travel vs Path of Travel
  b) back elbow - which introduces the following:
   i) Striking with an upper body natural weapon, other than the hand
   ii) reversing the line of another maneuver
  c) uppercut punch - which introduces the following:
   i) no rotation of the hand during the delivery of a punch

4) The following new blocks:
  a) push-down block - which introduces the following:
   i) blocking with the tip of the weapon (hand)
   ii) opening the hand for defense

5) The concept of shifting from a Reverse Bow to a specialized Horse. This sets the concepts that the practitioner must learn:
  a) new degree of rotation to achieve same effects as shifting from Neutral Bow to Forward Bow
  b) to establish a base before executing a strike (elbow)

6) The concept of stepping forward with a cover step. This sets the concepts that the practitioner must learn:
  a) preview of next form - Short Form Two

7) The concept of an intersection position. This sets the concepts that the practitioner must learn:
  a) preview of next form - Short Form Two

8) The concept of a call out or highlighted maneuver. This sets the concept that specific maneuvers are emphasized within the form to draw attention to the information they present. The call out moves of this form are:
  a) 45 degree cat stance with covering block
  b) back elbow strike
  c) stepping forward with a block

Analysis of Long Form One   207

9)
    d) isolation

10)
    The concept of rotating to a forward bow with out the lower body (legs / feet)

    The concept of Isolation maneuvers. This sets the concepts that the practitioner must learn:
        a) isolation maneuvers are designed as maneuvers which the practitioner must contemplate on to find their true purpose in the form - i.e. not all information is given to the practitioner about the meaning of these maneuvers

---

Long Form One falls into the category of a dictionary form. As such, it maintains the following elements of the dictionary forms.

1)
    Each dictionary form changes the foot pattern on the first downward block.

Short Form One has a number of other elements it teaches:

1)
    It continues the category completion of Torque when compared with Short Form One

---

© 2014 EPAKS Publications

Reverse / Opposite

Note:
> This analysis is limited to only the new basics contained in Long Form One and the basics that were extended upon from Short Form One. It does not include basics that are in future forms.

Blocks

    Right Thrusting Inward Block
        Reverses
            None
        Opposites
            Rear Hand / Front Hand Block
            Right Hammering Inward Block
            Left Block
            Left Inward Block
            Hammering Inward Block
            Outward Block
            Strike
            Left / Right Straight Punch
            Left Back Elbow
            Left / Right Uppercut Punch

    Left Hammering Inward Block
        Reverses
            None
        Opposites
            Rear Hand / Front Hand Block
            Left Thrusting Inward Block
            Right Block
            Right Inward Block
            Thrusting Inward Block
            Outward Block
            Strike
            Left / Right Straight Punch
            Left Back Elbow
            Left / Right Uppercut Punch

    Left Vertical Outward Block
        Reverses
            Right Vertical Outward Block
            Left Covering Inward Block
        Opposites
            Rear Hand / Front Hand Block
            Right Block
            Inward Block
            Outside Downward Block

    Strike
        Left / Right Straight Punch
        Left Back Elbow
        Left / Right Uppercut Punch

Right Vertical Outward Block
    Reverses
        Left Vertical Outward Block
        Right Covering Inward Block
    Opposites
        Rear Hand / Front Hand Block
        Left Block
        Left Vertical Outward Block
        Inward Block
        Outside Downward Block
    Strike
        Left / Right Straight Punch
        Left Back Elbow
        Left / Right Uppercut Punch

Left Upward Block
    Reverses
        None
    Opposites
        Rear Hand / Front Hand Block
        Right Block
        Right Upward Block
        Downward Block
    Strike
        Left / Right Straight Punch
        Left Back Elbow
        Left / Right Uppercut Punch

Right Upward Block
    Reverses
        None
    Opposites
        Rear Hand / Front Hand Block
        Left Block
        Left Upward Block
        Downward Block

Analysis of Long Form One

      Strike
      Left / Right Straight Punch
      Left Back Elbow
      Left / Right Uppercut Punch

Right (Outside) Downward Block
    Reverses
      Right Inside Downward Block (Palm Down / Palm Down)
      Left Outside Downward Block
    Opposites
      Rear Hand / Front Hand Block
      Left Block
      Upward Block
      Vertical Outward Block
      Strike
      Left / Right Straight Punch
      Left Back Elbow
      Left / Right Uppercut Punch

Left (Outside) Downward Block
    Reverses
      Left Inside Downward Block (Palm Down / Palm Up)
      Right Outside Downward Block
    Opposites
      Rear Hand / Front Hand Block
      Right Block
      Upward Block
      Vertical Outward Block
      Strike
      Left / Right Straight Punch
      Left Back Elbow
      Left / Right Uppercut Punch

Left (Inside) Downward Block
    Reverses
      Right Outside Downward Block
    Opposites
      Right Inside Downward Block (Palm Down / Palm Up)

Right Block
Upward Block
Vertical Outward Block
Palm up / Palm Down
Strike
Left / Right Straight Punch
Left Back Elbow
Left / Right Uppercut Punch

Right (Inside) Downward Block
    Reverses
        Left Outside Downward Block
    Opposites
        Left Inside Downward Block (Palm Down / Palm Up)
        Right Block
        Upward Block
        Vertical Outward Block
        Palm up / Palm Down
        Strike
        Left / Right Straight Punch
        Left Back Elbow
        Left / Right Uppercut Punch

Left Push-Down Block
    Reverses
        Left / Right Uppercut Punch
    Opposites
        Right Block
        Upward Block
        Strike
        Left / Right Straight Punch
        Left Back Elbow
        Left / Right Uppercut Punch

Right Push-Down Block
    Reverses
        Left / Right Uppercut Punch
    Opposites
        Left Block
        Upward Block

Analysis of Long Form One

Strike
Left / Right Straight Punch
Left Back Elbow
Left / Right Uppercut Punch

Strikes

    Left Straight Punch
        Reverses
            Left Back Elbow
        Opposites
            Right Strike
            Right Straight Punch
            Left / Right 45 degree Punch
            Left / Right 90 degree Punch
            Left / Right Uppercut Punch
            Block
            Left / Right Inward Block
            Left / Right Vertical Outward Block
            Left / Right Upward Block
            Left / Right Outside Downward Block
            Left / Right Inside Downward Block (Palm up / Palm Down)
            Left / Right Push-Down Block

    Right Straight Punch
        Reverses
            None
        Opposites
            Left Strike
            Left Straight Punch
            Left / Right 45 degree Punch
            left / Right 90 degree Punch
            Left / Right Uppercut Punch
            Block
            Left / Right Inward Block
            Left / Right Vertical Outward Block
            Left / Right Upward Block
            Left / Right Outside Downward Block
            Left / Right Inside Downward Block (Palm up / Palm Down)
            Left / Right Push-Down Block

    Left Side Elbow
        Reverses

Analysis of Long Form One — 215

    Left Straight Punch
    Opposites
        Right Strike
        Right Straight Punch
        Left / Right 45 degree Punch
        Left / Right 90 degree Punch
        Left / Right Uppercut Punch
        Block
        Left / Right Inward Block
        Left / Right Vertical Outward Block
        Left / Right Upward Block
        Left / Right Outside Downward Block
        Left / Right Inside Downward Block (Palm up / Palm Down)
        Left / Right Push-Down Block

Left 45 degree Punch
    Reverses
        None
    Opposites
        Right Strike
        Right 45 degree Punch
        Left / Right Straight Punch
        Left / Right 90 degree Punch
        Left / Right Uppercut Punch
        Block
        Left / Right Inward Block
        Left / Right Vertical Outward Block
        Left / Right Upward Block
        Left / Right Outside Downward Block
        Left / Right Inside Downward Block (Palm up / Palm Down)
        Left / Right Push-Down Block

Right 45 degree Punch
    Reverses
        None
    Opposites
        Left Strike
        Left 45 degree Punch
        Left / Right Straight Punch

© 2014 EPAKS Publications

　　　　Left / Right 90 degree Punch
　　　　Left / Right Uppercut Punch
　　　　Block
　　　　Left / Right Inward Block
　　　　Left / Right Vertical Outward Block
　　　　Left / Right Upward Block
　　　　Left / Right Outside Downward Block
　　　　Left / Right Inside Downward Block (Palm up / Palm Down)
　　　　Left / Right Push-Down Block

　　Left 90 degree Punch
　　　　Reverses
　　　　　　Right 90 degree Punch
　　　　Opposites
　　　　　　Right Strike
　　　　　　Right 90 degree Punch
　　　　　　Left / Right 45 degree Punch
　　　　　　Left / Right Straight Punch
　　　　　　Left / Right Uppercut Punch
　　　　　　Block
　　　　　　Left / Right Inward Block
　　　　　　Left / Right Vertical Outward Block
　　　　　　Left / Right Upward Block
　　　　　　Left / Right Outside Downward Block
　　　　　　Left / Right Inside Downward Block (Palm up / Palm Down)
　　　　　　Left / Right Push-Down Block

　　Right 90 degree Punch
　　　　Reverses
　　　　　　Left 90 degree Punch
　　　　Opposites
　　　　　　Left Strike
　　　　　　Left 90 degree Punch
　　　　　　Left / Right 45 degree Punch
　　　　　　Left / Right Straight Punch
　　　　　　Left / Right Uppercut Punch
　　　　　　Block
　　　　　　Left / Right Inward Block

Analysis of Long Form One

Left / Right Vertical Outward Block
Left / Right Upward Block
Left / Right Outside Downward Block
Left / Right Inside Downward Block (Palm up / Palm Down)
Left / Right Push-Down Block

Foot Maneuvers

Left Step Through Reverse
    Reverses
        None
    Opposites
        Right Step Through Reverse
        Cover

Right Step Through Reverse
    Reverses
        None
    Opposites
        Left Step Through Reverse
        Cover

Left 90 Degree Cover
    Reverses
        Right 90 Degree Cover
    Opposites
        Cover (close distance)
        Right 90 Degree Cover
        180 Degree Cover
        Step Through

Right 180 Degree Cover
    Reverses
        Left 180 Degree Cover
    Opposites
        Cover (close distance)
        Left 180 Degree Cover
        90 Degree Cover
        Step Through

Left 180 Degree Cover
    Reverses
        Right 180 Degree Cover
    Opposites
        Cover (close distance)
        Right 180 Degree Cover
        90 Degree Cover

Analysis of Long Form One | **219**

Step Through

Body Maneuvers

Shift forward (into Forward Bow - with lower body)
    Reverses
        None
    Opposites
        Shift forward (without Forward Bow - without lower body)

Torque Analysis Only - Triple Block Section Only

Shift backward with Inward Block (Direct Rotational)
    Reverses
        Shift backward with Inward Block (opposite side)
        Shift forward with Inward Block (same side)
        Step Through reverse with Inward Block
        Shift forward with Vertical Outward Block (opposite side)
        Shift backward with Vertical Outward Block (opposite side)
        90 degree Cover with Downward Block
        Shift forward with Downward Block (same side)
        Shift backward with Downward Block (opposite side)
        Step Through reverse with Downward Block
    Opposites
        Shift forward with Inward Block (opposite side)
        Step Through reverse with Vertical Outward Block
        Shift forward with Left Vertical Outward Block
        Step Through reverse with Vertical Outward Block
        Shift backward with Left Vertical Outward Block
        Shift backward with Left Downward Block
        Shift forward with Left Downward Block

Shift forward with Right Inward Block (Direct Rotational)
    Reverses
        Shift backward in Inward Block (same side)
        Shift forward with Inward Block (opposite side)
        90 degree Cover with Vertical Outward Block
        Shift forward with Vertical Outward Block (opposite side)
        Shift backward with Vertical Outward Block (opposite side)
        Shift backward with Downward Block (same side)
        Shift forward with Downward Block (opposite side)
    Opposites
        Step Through reverse with Inward Block
        Shift backward with Right Inward Block
        Shift backward with Right Vertical Outward Block
        Shift forward with Left Vertical Outward Block

90 degree cover with Downward Block
Shift forward with Right Downward Block
Step Through reverse with Downward
Shift backward with Right Downward

Step Through reverse with Inward Block (Direct Rotational)
Reverses
Shift forward with Right Inward Block
Shift backward with Inward Block (opposite side)
Shift forward with Inward Block (same side)
90 degree Cover with Vertical Outward Block
Shift forward with Vertical Outward Block (same side)
Step Through reverse with Vertical Outward Block
Shift backward with Vertical Outward Block (opposite side)
Shift backward with Downward Block (opposite side)
Shift forward with Downward Block (same side)
Opposites
Shift forward with Left Inward Block
Shift backward with Right Vertical Outward Block
Shift forward with Left Vertical Outward Block
90 degree cover with Downward Block
Shift forward with Right Downward Block
Step Through reverse with Downward
Shift backward with Right Downward

Shift forward with Left Inward Block (Direct Rotational)
Reverses
Shift forward with Inward Block (opposite side)
Step Through reverse with Inward Block
Shift backward with Inward Block (same side)
Shift backward with Vertical Outward Block (same side)
Shift forward with Vertical Outward Block (opposite side)
90 degree Cover with Downward Block
Shift forward with Downward Block (opposite side)
Step Through reverse with Downward Block
Shift backward with Downward Block (same side)

Opposites
    Shift backward with Left Inward Block
    90 degree cover with Vertical Outward Block
    90 degree cover with Downward Block
    Shift forward with Left Vertical Outward Block
    Step Through reverse with Vertical Outward Block
    Shift backward with Left Vertical Outward Block
    Shift backward with Left Downward Block
    Step Through reverse with Downward Block
    Shift backward with Right Downward Block

Shift backward with Right Inward Block (Direct Rotational)
    Reverses
        Shift backward with Inward Block (opposite side)
        Shift forward with Inward Block (same side)
        90 degree Cover with Vertical Outward Block
        Shift forward with Vertical Outward Block (same side)
        Step Through reverse with Vertical Outward Block
        Shift backward with Vertical Outward Block (opposite side)
        Shift backward with Downward Block (opposite side)
        Shift forward with Downward Block (same side)
    Opposites
        Shift forward with Left Inward Block
        Step Through reverse with Inward Block
        Shift backward with Right Vertical Outward Block
        Shift Forward with Right Vertical Outward Block
        90 degree cover with Downward Block
        Shift forward with Right Downward Block
        Step Through reverse with Downward
        Shift backward with Right Downward

90 degree Cover with Vertical Outward Block (Direct Rotational)
    Reverses
        Shift forward with Inward Block (opposite)
        Shift backward with Inward Block (same side)
        Shift backward with Vertical Outward Block (same side)

Shift forward with Vertical Outward Block (opposite side)
90 degree Cover with Downward Block
Shift forward with Downward Block (same side)
Step Through reverse with Downward Block
Shift backward with Downward Block (opposite side)
Opposites
  Shift backward with Left Inward Block
  Shift forward with Left Inward Block
  Shift forward with Right Left Vertical Outward Block
  Step Through reverse with Vertical Outward Block
  Shift backward with Left Vertical Outward Block
  Shift backward with Left Downward Block
  Shift forward with Left Downward Block

Shift forward with Left Vertical Outward Block (Counter Rotational)
Reverses
  Shift forward with Inward Block (opposite side)
  Step Through reverse with Inward Block
  Shift backward with Inward Block (same side)
  Shift backward with Vertical Outward Block (same side)
  Shift forward with Vertical Outward Block (opposite side)
  90 degree Cover with Downward Block
  Shift forward with Downward Block (opposite side)
  Step Through reverse with Downward Block
  Shift backward with Downward Block (same side)
Opposites
  Shift backward with Left Inward Block
  Shift forward with Left Inward Block
  90 degree Cover with Vertical Outward Block
  Step Through reverse with Vertical Outward Block
  Shift backward with Left Vertical Outward Block
  Shift backward with Left Downward Block
  Shift forward with Left Downward Block

© 2014 EPAKS Publications

Analysis of Long Form One 225

Shift backward with Right Vertical Outward Block (Counter Rotational)
    Reverses
        Shift backward with Inward Block (opposite side)
        Shift forward with Inward Block (same side)
        90 degree Cover with Vertical Outward Block
        Shift forward with Vertical Outward Block (same side)
        Step Through reverse with Vertical Outward Block
        Shift backward with Vertical Outward Block (opposite side)
        Shift backward with Downward Block (opposite side)
        Shift forward with Downward Block (same side)
    Opposites
        Shift forward with Right Inward Block
        Step Through reverse with Inward Block
        Shift backward with Right Inward Block
        Shift forward with Right Vertical Outward Block
        90 degree Cover with Downward Block
        Shift forward with Right Downward Block
        Step Through reverse with Downward Block
        Shift backward with Right Downward Block

Step Through reverse with Vertical Outward Block (Counter Rotational)
    Reverses
        Shift forward with Inward Block (same side)
        Shift backward with Inward Block (opposite side)
        Shift backward with Vertical Outward Block (opposite side)
        Shift forward with Vertical Outward Block (same side)
        90 degree Cover with Downward Block
        Shift forward with Downward Block (same side)
        Step Through reverse with Downward Block
        Shift backward with Downward Block (opposite side)
    Opposites
        Shift backward with Left Inward Block
        Shift forward with Right Inward Block

© 2014 EPAKS Publications

90 degree Cover with Vertical Outward Block
Shift forward with Left Vertical Outward Block
Shift backward with Left Vertical Outward Block
Shift backward with Left Downward Block
Shift forward with Left Downward Block

Upward Blocks
   Reverses
     NA
   Opposites
     NA

90 degree Cover with Downward Block (Direct Rotational)
   Reverses
     Shift backward with Inward Block (same side)
     Shift forward with Inward Block (opposite side)
     90 degree Cover with Vertical Outward Block
     Shift forward with Vertical Outward Block (opposite side)
     Step Through reverse with Vertical Outward Block
     Shift backward with Vertical Outward Block (same side)
     Shift backward with Downward Block (same side)
     Shift forward with Downward Block (opposite side)
   Opposites
     Shift forward with Right inward Block
     Shift backward with Right Inward Block
     Shift backward with Right Vertical Outward Block
     Shift forward with Right Vertical Outward Block
     90 degree Cover with Downward Block
     Shift forward with Right Downward Block
     Shift backward with Right Downward Block

Shift forward with Downward Block (Counter Rotational)
   Reverses
     Shift backward with Inward Block (same side)
     Shift forward with Inward Block (opposite side)
     90 degree Cover with Vertical Outward Block
     Shift forward with Vertical Outward Block (opposite side)
     Step Through reverse with Vertical Outward Block

Shift backward with Vertical Outward Block (same side)
Shift backward with Downward Block (same side)
Shift forward with Downward Block (opposite side)
  Opposites
    Shift forward with Right Inward Block
    Shift backward with Right Inward Block
    Shift backward with Right Vertical Outward Block
    Shift forward with Right Vertical Outward Block
    90 degree Cover with Downward Block
    Shift backward with Right Downward Block
    Step Through reverse with Downward Block
    Shift backward with Right Downward Block

Shift backward with Downward Block (Counter Rotational)
  Reverses
    Shift forward with Inward Block (same side)
    Shift backward with Inward Block (opposite side)
    Shift backward with Vertical Outward Block (opposite side)
    Shift forward with Vertical Outward Block (same side)
    90 degree Cover with Downward Block
    Shift forward with Downward Block (same side)
    Step Through reverse with Downward Block
    Shift backward with Downward Block (opposite side)
  Opposites
    Shift backward with Left Inward Block
    Shift forward with Right Inward Block
    90 degree Cover with Vertical Outward Block
    Shift forward with Left Vertical Outward Block
    Step Through reverse with Vertical Outward Block
    Shift backward with Left Vertical Outward Block
    Shift forward with Left Downward Block

Step Through reverse with Downward Block (Counter Rotational)
  Reverses
    Shift backward with Inward Block (opposite side)
    Shift forward with Inward Block (same side)

90 degree Cover with Vertical Outward Block
Shift backward with Vertical Outward Block (opposite side)
Step Through reverse with Vertical Outward Block
Shift backward with Vertical Outward Block (opposite side)
Shift backward with Downward Block (opposite side)
Shift forward with Downward Block (same side)
  Opposites
Shift forward with Right Inward Block
Step Through reverse with Inward Block
Shift backward with Right Inward Block
Shift backward with Right Vertical Outward Block
Shift forward with Right Vertical Outward Block
90 degree Cover with Downward Block
Shift forward with Right Downward Block
Shift backward with Right Downward Block

Shift forward with Downward Block (Counter Rotational)
  Reverses
Shift forward with Inward Block (opposite side)
Shift backward with Inward Block (same side)
Shift backward with Vertical Outward Block (same side)
Shift forward with Vertical Outward Block (opposite side)
90 degree Cover with Downward Block
Shift forward with Downward Block (opposite side)
Step Through reverse with Downward Block
Shift backward with Downward Block (same side)
  Opposites
Shift backward with Left Inward Block
Shift forward with Right Inward Block
90 degree Cover with Vertical Outward Block
Shift forward with Left Vertical Outward Block
Step Through reverse with Vertical Outward Block
Shift backward with Left Vertical Outward Block
Shift backward with Left Downward Block

Shift backward with Downward Block (Counter Rotational)

Analysis of Long Form One   229

Reverses
    Shift backward with Inward Block (opposite side)
    Shift forward with Inward Block (same side)
    90 degree Cover with Vertical Outward Block
    Shift forward with Vertical Outward Block (same side)
    Step Through reverse with Vertical Outward Block
    Shift backward with Vertical Outward Block (opposite side)
    Shift backward with Downward Block (opposite side)
    Shift forward with Downward Block (same side)
Opposites
    Shift forward with Right Inward Block
    Step Through reverse with Inward Block
    Shift backward with Right Inward Block
    Shift backward with Right Vertical Outward Block
    Shift forward with Right Vertical Outward Block
    90 degree Cover with Downward Block
    Shift forward with Right Downward Block
    Step Through reverse with Right Downward Block

Principles / Rules / Theories / Concepts / Definitions

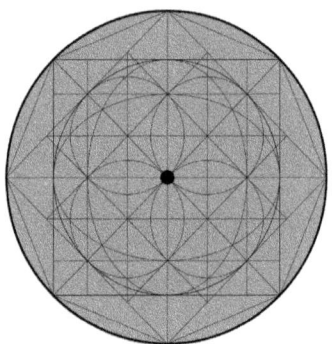

Dictionary

Advance, Align, Angle, Anchor, Attacker, Attention, Attitude, Available, Balance, Ball, Base, Block, Bounce, Bow, Break, Breathe, Category, Center-line, Chamber, Circle, Cock, Concept, Contact, Contour, Coordination, Counter, Cover, Defense, Deflect, Deliver, Depth, Deviate, Diagonal, Dictionary, Dimension, Direct, Direction, Disharmony, Distance, Downward, Embryonic, Environment, Execute, Exhale, Focus, Force, Form, Forward, Front, Gap, Gauge, Guide, Hammer, Hard, Harm, Harmony, Height, Hide, Hidden, Horizontal, Hurt, Idea, Inhale, Inside, Intent, Intentional, Intercept, Intersect, Intersection, Inward, Isolation, Kata, Lever, Leverage, Line, Major, Maneuver, Mechanical, Meditation, Meet, Method, Minor, Minus, Motion, Move, Mumble, Neutral, Offense, Opponent, Opposite, Outer, Outward, Path, Penetration, Pivot, Plane, Plant, Plus, Position, Posture, Power, Practice, Practitioner, Prevent, Primitive, Principle, Pronounce, Proportional, Protect, Punch, Range, Rank, Read, Rear, Rearrange, Redirect, Regulate, Relax, Retract, Reverse, Rhythm, Rotate, Rule, Salutation, Saying, Scan, School, Sensei, Set, Settle, Shape, Shift, Side, Signify, Simultaneous, Slide, Soft, Solidify, Sophisticated, Space, Speed, Square,

Analysis of Long Form One | 231

Stable, Stationary, Step, Strike, Student, Studio, Style, Survey, Switch, Symmetrical, Sync, Synchronize, System, Tactic, Tailor, Target, Telegraph, Theory, Thrust, Timing, Tip, Torque, Touch, Tournament, Traditional, Train, Transitory, Travel, Turn, Unify, Unuseful, Upward, Use, Useless, Velocity, Vertical, Viewpoint, Weapon, Width, With, X, Yield, Zone

Terms

8 Major Angles of Attack, 8 Major Angles of Balance, 8 Major Angles of Defense, Accumulated Force, Alphabet of Motion, Anatomical Positioning, Anatomical Weak Point, Angle Alignment, Angle of Attack, Angle of Avoidance, Angle of Balance, Angle of Contact, Angle of Cover, Angle of Defense, Angle of Deflection, Angle of Delivery, Angle of Departure, Angle of Deviation, Angle of Efficiency, Angle of Execution, Angle if Incidence, Angle of Obscurity, Angle of Prevention, Angle of Protection, Angle of Retraction, Angle of Travel, Articulation of Motion, Axis of Rotation, Back-up Mass, Body Alignment, Body Harmony, Body Fusion, Body Mechanics, Body Momentum, Body Rotation, Body Settle, Brace Angle, Break the Heel, Broken Rhythm, Category Completion, Center of Gravity, Center of Mass, Chambered Position, Changing the Guard, Circular Confinement, Clock Principle, Close the Gap, Close the Gate, Close the Line, Close Range, Close Range Weapon, Colliding Forces, Compact Unit, Completed Path of Travel, Conceptual Box, Contact Deviation, Contact Penetration, Contour Confinement, Contour Guidance, Corrective Adjustment, Cover Step, Defensive Defense, Defensive Reaction, Degree of Attack, Degree of Contact, Degree of Intent, Degree of Rotation, Delayed Movement, Depth of Action, Depth Penetration, Depth Perception, Depth Zone, Diagonal Plane, Dimensional Zone, Direct Opposites, Directional Harmony, Directional Movement, Directional Switch, Disharmony of Travel, Disharmony of Force, Disrupted Rhythm, Double Factor, Economy of Motion, Environmental Awareness, Environmental Condition, Establish your Base, Explosive Action, Field of View, Filling the Gap, Fluid

Movement, Form Indicator, Forward Back-up Mass, Frozen Motion, Gauging Leg, General Rule, Geometric Angle, Geometric Line, Geometric Path, Harmonious Movement, Harmonized Power, Heel-Knee Alignment, Heel-Toe Alignment, Height Zone, Horizontal Plane, Horizontal Punch, Horizontal Zone, Horizontal Zone of Attack, Horizontal Zone of Defense, Horizontal Zone of Protection, In Sync, In-Place, Intercepting Forces, Intersecting Action, Intersecting Forces, Invisible Box, Jet Lag, Line of Action, Line of Attack, Line of Defense, Line of Delivery, Line of Execution, Line of Sight, Line of Travel, Lock-Out, Long Form, Long Range, Long Range Weapon, Lower Case, Maintain the Gap, Margin for Error, Medium Range, Medium Range Weapon, Mental Distraction, Mental Harmony, Method of Attack, Method of Defense, Method of Delivery, Method of Execution, Method of Travel, Mirror Image, Motion Analysis, Movement of Punctuation, Natural Defenses, Natural Weapon, Neutral Zone of Defense, Obscure Zone, Offensive Offense, Open the Gap, Open the Gate, Open the Line, Opposing Forces, Opposite Motion, Optimum Angle of Incidence, Outer Rim, Over Rotate, Over Reach, Over Rotate, Path of Action, Path of Attack, Path of Defense, Path of Delivery, Path of Entry, Path of Execution, Path of Retraction, Path of Travel, Penetration Point, Peripheral Assessment, Peripheral Awareness, Peripheral Registering, Peripheral Scan, Peripheral Vision, Physical Harmony, Physical Preparedness, Physical Speed, Pivot Point, Pivoting Axis, Placement of Target, Point of Cancellation, Point of Contact, Point of Impact, Point of Origin, Point of Pivot, Point of Reference, Positional Alignment, Positional Cock, Positional Cover, Positioned Block, Postural Position, Power Principle, Proportional Dimension, Proportional Execution, Protective Measure, Reference Point, Residual Torque, Return Motion, Reverse Motion, Reverse Punch, Rotating Axis, Rotating Force, Rotational Velocity, Self-correcting, Settle into Balance, Short Form, Short Range, Short Range Weapon, Solidify your Base, Stabilize your Base, Step Back, Target Area, Target Availability, Target Placement, Toe-Heel Alignment, Toe-Toe Alignment, Toe-Toe Heel-Heel Alignment, Total Harmony, Total Mental Harmony, Total Physical Harmony, Transitional Move, Upper Case, Useless, V Step, Vertical Plane, Visual Interpretation, Vital Area, Vital Target,

Analysis of Long Form One   233

Wasted Motion, Weapon Alignment, Weapon Availability, Weight Distribution, Width Zone, Zone of Confinement, Zone of Obscurity, Zone of Protection

© 2014 EPAKS Publications

Chapter 8 - Improving Your Execution of Long Form One

There is a lot of subtle and often overlooked execution information that can be learned from Long Form One. The vast majority of this information is absorbed through perfecting the form through practice and through feedback from an instructor. Often this feedback and 'perfecting' is minute and absorbed through repetition and repeated correction. Also, this information is often absorbed over a long period of time, over a large number of practice sessions, and gets almost to the point that the information is absorbed subconsciously. To quote an often used phrase - 'One cannot fool experience'.

Improving Your Execution of Long Form One   235

Also, perfecting the execution of the other American Kenpo forms can help improve the execution of Long Form One. Therefore, it is not recommended that the practitioner preclude the practice of the other forms for this one. The diverse movements of the other forms can and will help to improve the execution of the seemingly simplistic maneuvers of this form.

Even though Long Form One is a relatively basic form, the skilled eye can easily discern differences between practiced and knowledgeable executions, from those that are more primitive and/or less experienced. Timing, elimination of wasted motion, settling, power, and smooth execution are only some of the factors that comprise a properly executed form.

General Errors

a) improper timing:
   i) double factor is not executed with initial foot contact of maneuver
   ii) major block is not timed with the settle into stance
   iii) punch is not executed with stance shift from Neutral Bow to Forward Bow

b) not turning head to new direction prior to foot maneuver

c) not looking straight ahead – i.e. looking up, down or wondering eyes

d) improper breathing:
   i) holding breath
   ii) breathing in during execution of major blocks

Timing

Timing is the coordination of multiple movements such that they are synchronized as intended. This definition is demonstrated throughout the form by timing both foot maneuvers (lower body) with blocks (upper body) in such a way as to create harmonious and fluid maneuvers which complete their execution in-sync with one another. With experience and practice, one can easily see correctly timed maneuvers from incorrectly timed maneuvers.

With the addition of stance shifting while executing offensive maneuvers, timing becomes slightly more complicated than with Short Form One. Creating harmonious movements timed such that the intended Focus Point of the strike is reached in-sync with the completion of body rotation along with the weight shift is of critical importance. Directional Harmony, Body Harmony, Body Alignment, Focus, and timing are needed to create a proper Confluence of Forces.

Gaze

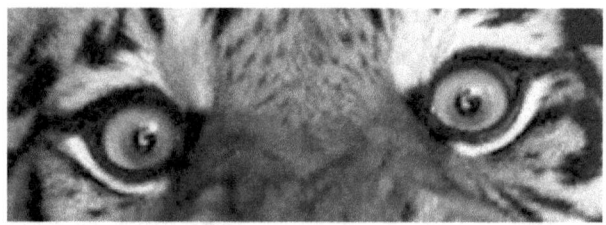

The look on a practitioner's face and specifically the look in their eyes can heavily influence the perception of how a form is perceived. It is said that the eyes are the window to the soul. One can use this adage to their advantage to manipulate the viewer's perception of one's performance. This along with the practitioner's attitude can go a long way to overcoming other short-falls that may occur in their form execution.

During the execution of Long Form One, the practitioner should always keep their gaze at eye level and parallel to the floor. This practice helps in maintaining a straight back and well balanced stance. Also, it is a general rule to always look into the direction one is intending to step before executing the foot maneuver. This should be done by not only shifting the eyes, but also turning the head.

Breathing

Breathing is an important part of the execution of any maneuver in American Kenpo. Long Form One is no exception. One must learn the importance of breath and how it affects their performance.

One bad habit that numerous beginner to intermediate students sometimes pick up is the holding of their breath during the execution of maneuvers. This should be corrected by having the practitioner concentrate on smooth and relaxed breathing. The only emphasis in one's breath should be at the anticipated point of contact of the defensive or offensive maneuver. This emphasis of breath should be for the purpose of helping to focus one's energy. Holding one's breath can lead to Constipated Motion - i.e. motion that is not fluid and/or smooth, but rather staccato and/or stiff in nature.

The kiai is a form of focusing one's breath by creating an audible sound with the breath through tightening of the abdominal muscles, thus forcing the breath to exhale. Some instructors teach using kiais to help students focus their breath with their maneuvers. Although Long Form One does not specifically contain any kiais in it's standard execution, it is not an incorrect nor bad teaching tool. On the contrary, it can be used to help a student correct breathing issues, along with teaching the purpose of tightening muscles in anticipation of absorbing an oncoming strike to the body. It can also be used as an 'attention getter' when executing a form in competition.

Stances

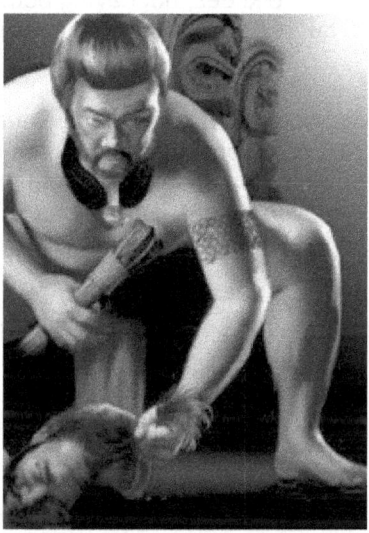

Stances are the base of our execution. Stances can be loosely defined as frozen motion. Without properly articulated stances, the execution of Long Form One can never be perfected. The most commonly overlooked item among stances is proper positioning. Positioning includes a large number of elements. These include foot/leg alignments, body alignments, and arm/hand alignments. One should become comfortable with the knowledge of proper alignments and dimensions of the stances. This cannot be overstated. The proper dimensions and alignments of each of the stances is highlighted in detail in SGM Parker's book, "Infinite Insights into Kenpo - book #2 (Physical Analyzation I)."

Long Form One, being one of the first forms of the system, exposes only six stances during it's execution (not including the salutation): the Meditating Horse, Neutral Bow, Forward Bow, 45 degree Cat, Fighting Horse, and Reverse Bow.

© 2014 EPAKS Publications

Some of the most common mistakes of the Meditating Horse are: not having the toes point directly ahead (or slightly inward), not bending the knees, not having both elbows point downward at a 45 degree angle, and/or not keeping the back up straight.

Some of the most common mistakes of the Neutral Bow are: not having both feet point forward at 45 degree angle; not having the proper width (toe / heel alignment) or depth (heel / knee alignment), uneven weight distribution (50% / 50%), and/or not keeping the back up straight with the shoulders relaxed.

Some of the most common mistakes of the Forward Bow are: not having the rear foot pointing directly forward, not having the proper width (toe / heel alignment) or depth (heel / knee alignment), not having the rear foot flat on the ground, improper weight distribution (60% / 40%), and/or not keeping the back up straight with the shoulders relaxed.

Some of the most common mistakes of the 45 degree Cat are: not having the proper width (toe / heel alignment), improper weight distribution (10% / 90%), and/or not keeping the back up straight with the shoulders relaxed.

Some of the most common mistakes of the Fighting Horse are: not having the toes point directly to the side (in the same direction as the center-line), not bending the knees, and/or not keeping the back up straight.

Some of the most common mistakes of the Reverse Bow are: not having the front foot pointing to the rear at a 45 degree angle, not having the proper width (toe / heel alignment) or depth (heel / knee alignment), improper weight distribution (40% / 60%), and/or not keeping the back up straight with the shoulders relaxed.

Improving Your Execution of Long Form One

It is very common for the practitioner to start out with proper alignments, but quickly lose the alignments once any foot maneuvers are executed. One good exercise for drawing attention to the stances is to perform the entire form without the blocks and with hands on the hips. This exercise allows the practitioner to pay exclusive attention to the stances and foot maneuvers without having to split their attention on proper block execution.

Stance Errors

a) improper alignments
    i) foot width improper
    ii) foot depth improper
    iii) height improper (knees not bent enough or too much)

b) improper rotation for stance

c) improper weight distribution
    i) leaning in stance:
        1) leaning forward
        2) leaning side-to-side
    ii) shoulders not relaxed

d) improper arm/hand positioning

e) improper foot positioning

Improving Your Execution of Long Form One

Meditating Horse

a) proper alignments:
    i) toe/toe
    ii) heel/heel
    iii) slightly wider than shoulders

b) proper rotation:
    i) body faces directly forward
        1) hips on 3:00H - 9:00H line
        2) shoulders on 3:00H - 9:00H line
    ii) both feet face directly forward (or slightly inward)

c) proper weight distribution:
    i) 50/50

d) proper arm/hand positioning:
    i) hands placed at upper chest to chin level height

e) both feet placed completely flat

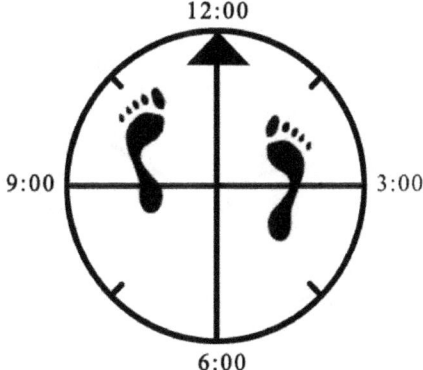

Example of bad toe-toe / heel - heel alignment for Horse

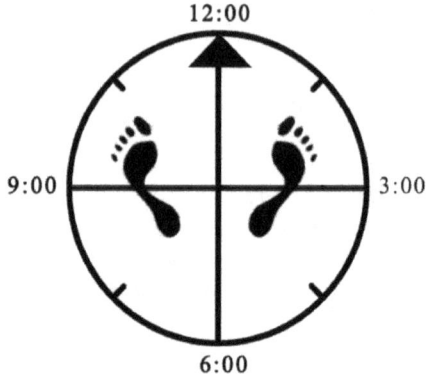

Example of toes pointing out for Horse

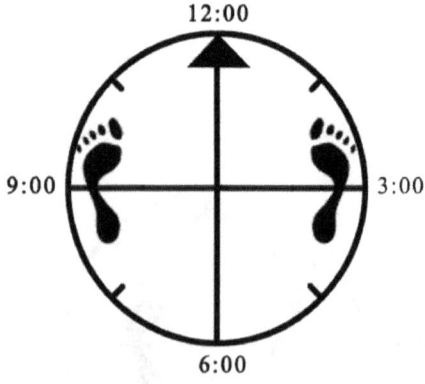

Example horse being too wide

Neutral Bow

a) proper alignments:
   i) toe/heel
   ii) heel/knee

b) proper rotation:
   i) body faces forward at 45 degrees
      1) hips on 10:30H - 4:30H or 1:30H - 7:30H line
      2) shoulders on 10:30H - 4:30H or 1:30H - 7:30H line
   ii) both feet point forward at 45 degrees (on 10:30H - 4:30H or 1:30H - 7:30H line)

c) proper weight distribution:
   i) 50/50

d) proper arm/hand positioning:
   i) unused arm in chambered position

e) both feet placed completely flat

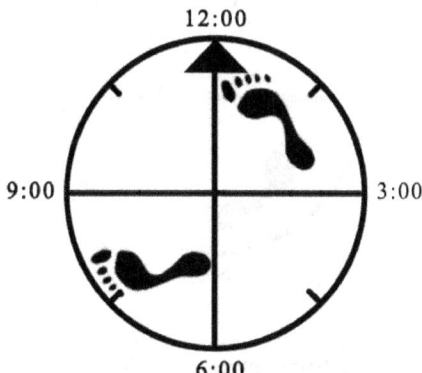

Example of bad rear foot angle for Neutral Bow

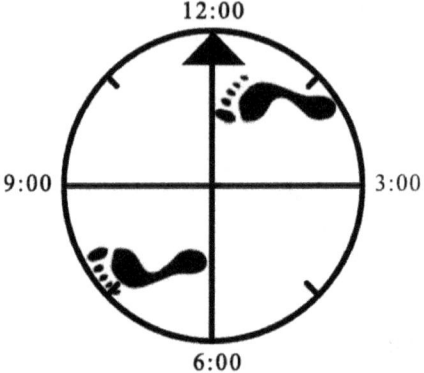

Example of bad foot angles (both) for Neutral Bow

Example of bad front foot angle for Neutral Bow

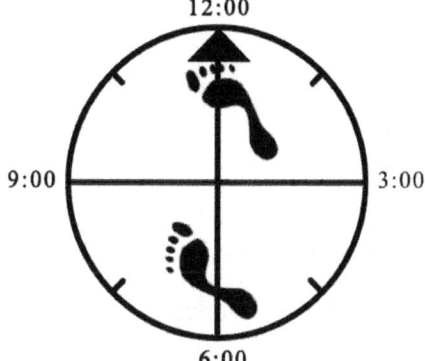

Example of improper width (narrow) for Neutral Bow

Forward Bow

a) proper alignments:
   i) toe/heel
   ii) heel/knee

b) proper rotation:
   i) body faces directly forward
      1) hips on 3:00H - 9:00H or 12:00H - 6:00H line
      2) shoulders on 3:00H - 9:00H or 12:00H - 6:00H line
   ii) front foot faces forward at 45 degrees (on 10:30H - 4:30H or 1:30H - 7:30H line)
   iii) rear foot faces directly forward

c) proper weight distribution:
   i) 60/40

d) proper arm/hand positioning:
   i) unused arm in chambered position

e) both feet placed completely flat

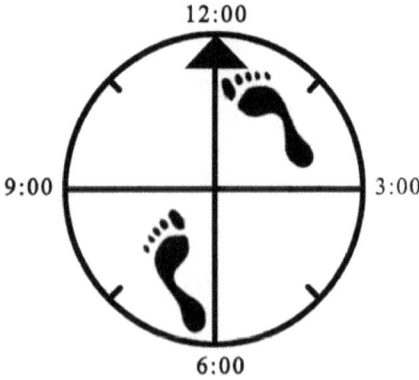

Example of bad rear foot angle for Forward Bow

© 2014 EPAKS Publications

Improving Your Execution of Long Form One — 251

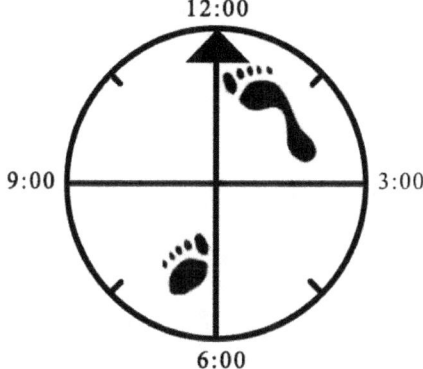

Example of rear heel not planted for Forward Bow

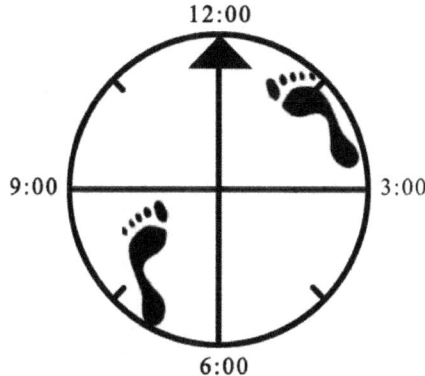

Example of improper width (wide) for Forward Bow

© 2014 EPAKS Publications

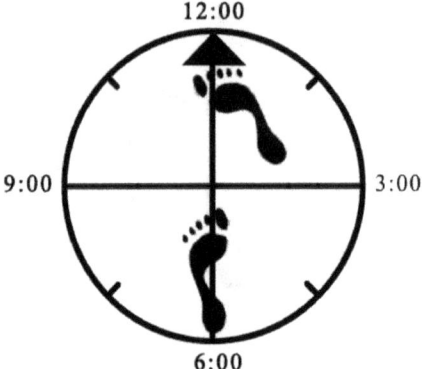

Example of improper width (narrow) for Neutral Bow

Improving Your Execution of Long Form One   253

45 degree Cat

a) proper alignments:
  i) toe/heel
  ii) 1 1/2 length of front foot from rear foot

b) proper rotation:
  i) body faces forward at 45 degrees
    1) hips on 10:30H - 4:30H or 1:30H - 7:30H line
    2) shoulders on 10:30H - 4:30H or 1:30H - 7:30H line
  ii) front foot faces directly forward - on ball of foot
  iii) rear foot faces forward at 45 degrees (on 10:30H - 4:30H or 1:30H - 7:30H line)

c) proper weight distribution:
  1) 10/90

d) proper arm/hand positioning:
  i) unused arm in chambered position

e) rear foot placed completely flat

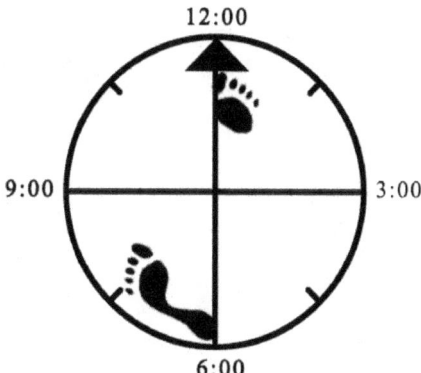

Example of bad rear foot angle for Neutral Bow

© 2014 EPAKS Publications

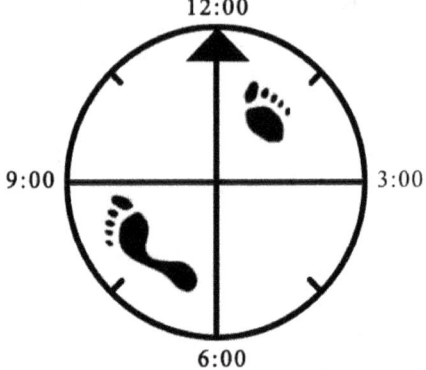

Example of bad foot angles (both) for Neutral Bow

Improving Your Execution of Long Form One 255

Reverse Bow

a) proper alignments:
   i) toe/heel
   ii) heel/knee

b) proper rotation:
   i) body faces backward at 45 degrees
      1) hips on 10:30H - 4:30H or 1:30H - 7:30H line
      2) shoulders on 10:30H - 4:30H or 1:30H - 7:30H line
   ii) front foot faces directly backward
   iii) rear foot faces backward at 45 degrees (on 10:30H - 4:30H or 1:30H - 7:30H line)

c) weight distribution:
   1) 40/60

d) proper arm/hand positioning:
   i) unused arm in chambered position

e) both feet placed completely flat

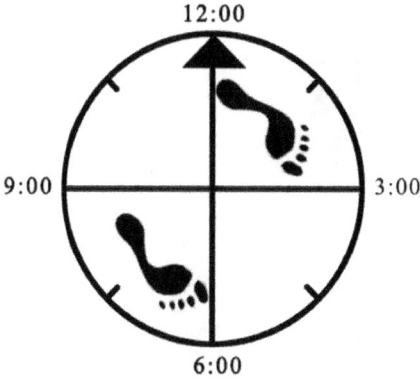

Example of bad front foot angle for Reverse Bow

© 2014 EPAKS Publications

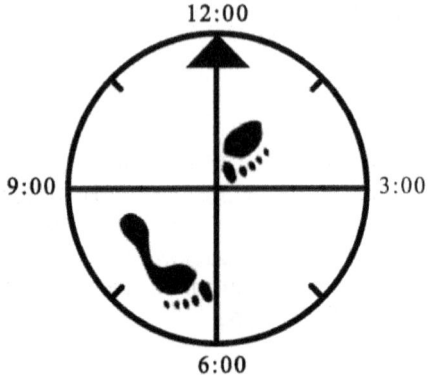

Example of front heel not planted for Reverse Bow

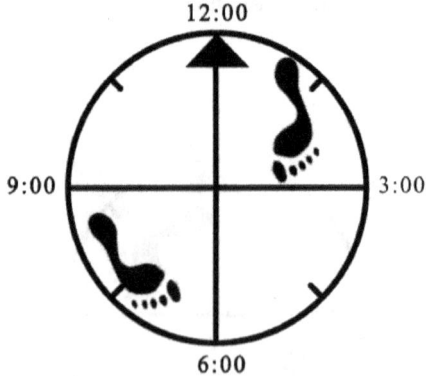

Example of improper width (wide) for Forward Bow

Improving Your Execution of Long Form One 257

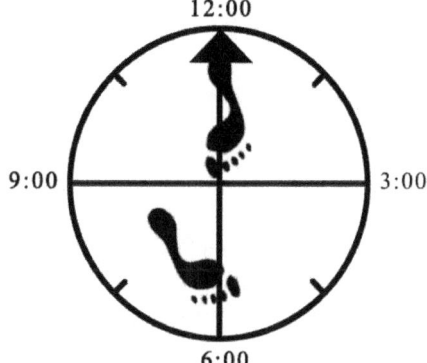

Example of improper width (narrow) for **Neutral Bow**

Fighting Horse

a) proper alignments:
    i) toe/toe
    ii) heel/heel
    iii) feet slightly wider than shoulders

b) proper rotation:
    i) body faces directly to side (perpendicular to Point of Reference)
        1) hips on 12:00H - 6:00H or 3:00H - 9:00H line
        2) shoulders on 12:00H - 6:00H or 3:00H - 9:00H line
    ii) both feet point directly to side (perpendicular to Point of Reference)

c) proper weight distribution:
    i) 50/50

d) proper arm/hand positioning:
    i) unused arm in chambered position

e) both feet placed completely flat

Improving Your Execution of Long Form One — 259

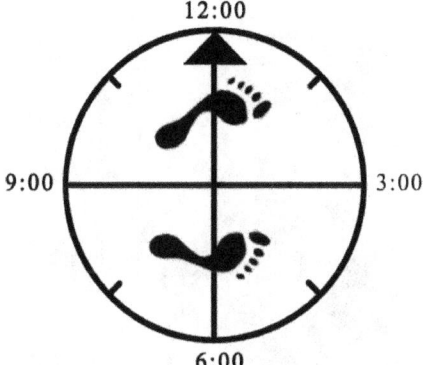

Example of bad front foot angle for Fighting Horse

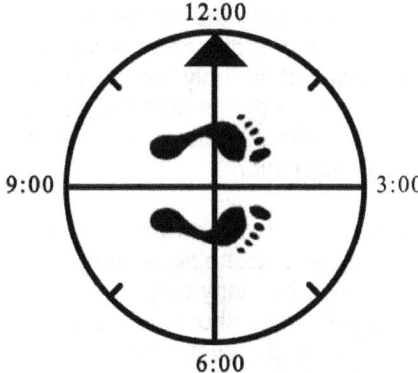

Example of improper depth (too shallow) for Fighting Horse

© 2014 EPAKS Publications

Foot Maneuvers

Foot maneuvers are basically the movement between stances. The improper execution of foot maneuvers can introduce a number of complexities of not only the movement itself, but also affect the new stance that is obtained at the end of the foot maneuver. The section on stance correction gives further highlights into this information.

There are a number of common errors exhibited while executing foot maneuvers. Bobbing is one of the most common problems demonstrated by many beginning practitioners. Transitions between stances should be fluid while also maintaining the same height level. Once Long Form One is started, the practitioner's head should remain at the same level throughout the entire execution of the form (including the Meditating Horse).

Improving Your Execution of Long Form One

Another common general error is extra motions, i.e. breaking the principle of Economy of Motion. This problem is exhibited in many forms, the most common of which are: moving the feet prior to actually executing the foot maneuver (extremely common), breaking the heel (lifting the heel) during step through maneuvers, pivoting on the heel of the foot, and/or Jet Lagging (leaning while stepping through).

Foot Maneuver Errors

a) not obeying Economy of Motion principle / Create a stable base rule:
    i) not stepping correctly:
        1) not stepping with correct foot
        2) not stepping directly to new location
        3) splitting the stance (moving both feet, instead of one)
    ii) creating too many adjustments with feet
    iii) bouncing up and down while executing foot maneuver or stationary

b) improper pivoting:
    i) rotating on the heel instead of the ball of the foot
    ii) rotating the incorrect foot - i.e. the wrong (or both feet)
    iii) under / over rotating - not rotating to the proper new angle
    iv) not properly rotating the upper body with the lower body

c) jet legging (splitting timing of lower/upper body – i.e. creating distance with feet first and then the upper body)

Improving Your Execution of Long Form One

Step Out to Meditating Horse

a) transition from Attention to Meditating Horse:
    i) stepping out with the right foot instead of the left
    ii) stepping to improper width (see stance errors section)
    iii) stepping to improper alignment (see stance errors section)

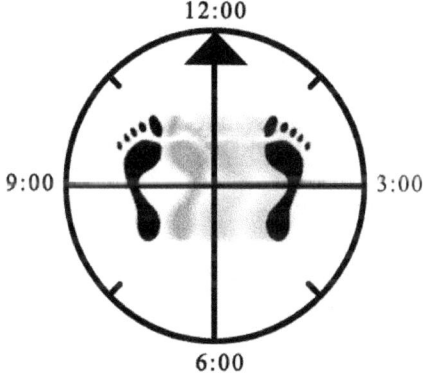

Example of stepping out with wrong foot into meditating Horse

Step Through

a) not obeying Economy of Motion principle / Create a stable base rule:
    i) creating too many adjustments with feet:
        1) breaking the heel (lifting/moving rear of foot before moving front of foot)
        2) adjusting/rotating feet prior to/during foot maneuvers
        3) adjusting the foot not used in a foot maneuver
        4) re-adjusting foot used in foot maneuver, after maneuver

b) improper pivoting:
    i) executing a twist through instead of a step through (splitting timing of distance/rotation during foot maneuver)

c) executing a cat stance as a separate motion – i.e. holding cat stance too long

Example of bobbing during a step through, reverse

Cover

a) stepping incorrectly:
  i) stepping with wrong foot

b) improper alignments:
  i) stepping to improper width (too narrow / too wide) (see stance errors section)
  ii) stepping to improper depth (too shallow / too deep) (see stance errors section)

c) improper pivoting:
  i) pivoting prior to completing the cover step (pivoting while stepping foot in air)

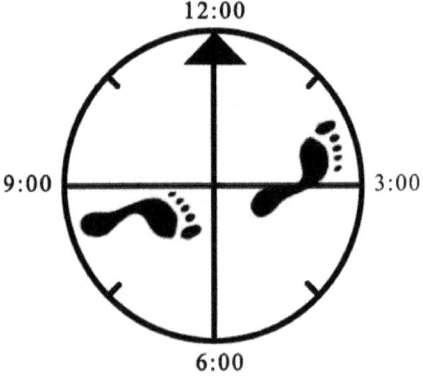

Example of improper width (narrow) for Cover Step

Improving Your Execution of Long Form One — 267

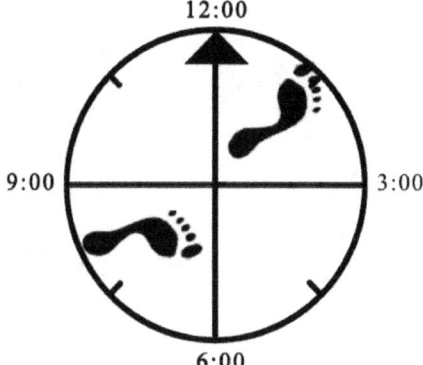

Example of improper width (wide) for Cover Step

Blocks

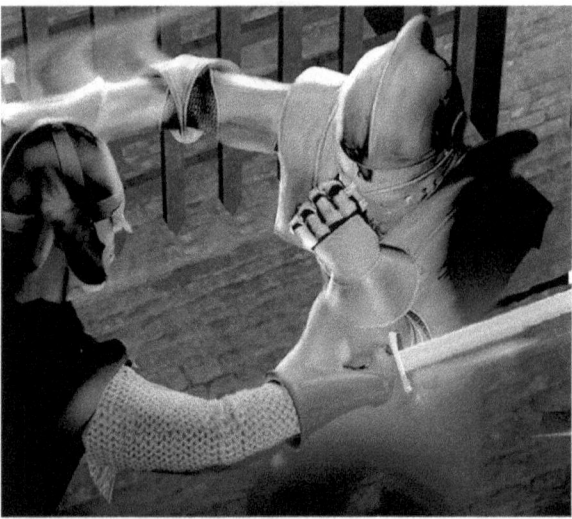

Blocking (defense) is one of the two major themes of Long Form One. Executing the blocks properly can make the difference between a successful defense and failure. Just like the stances, the practitioner should become intimately familiar with the proper dimensions utilized in each of the blocks. The primary concepts in dealing with blocking dimensions are the Outer Rim theory and/or the Invisible Box theory. These theories along with the proper dimensions for each block are highlighted in detail in SGM Parker's book, "Infinite Insights into Kenpo, book #3 (Physical Analyzation II)."

Some of the most common mistakes displayed while executing Long Form One blocks are: not executing the blocks to the proper dimensions; not executing the blocks to the proper angles; not executing the double factor block properly (especially the upward block); not executing the blocks efficiently (without Economy of Motion); and/or executing the block with improper timing.

Improving Your Execution of Long Form One

Block Errors

a) not obeying Economy of Motion principle:
   i) making a cock before execution of block
   ii) executing blocking outside the outer rim/invisible box

b) improper alignments:
   i) executed to improper dimensions

c) double factors:
   i) executed to improper dimensions

d) hand is not completely closed when executing blocks (minor and/or major)

e) not executing the blocks smoothly - i.e. mechanical / staccato motion

Inward Block

a) proper alignments:
    i) fist at eye-brow level
    ii) blocking arm extended to opposite shoulder
    iii) blocking arm extended to depth of Invisible Box
    iv) execution angle - forward at 45 degrees

b) executing two hammering inward blocks (instead of a hammering and thrusting)

Examples of bad Inward Blocks
(improper angle, width, and height - high / low)

Improving Your Execution of Long Form One

Vertical Outward Block

a) not obeying the rule of Margin for Error:
    ii) not anchoring the elbow
    iii) not keeping the vertical outward block vertical – i.e. over reaching

b) proper alignments:
    i) fist at eye-brow level
    ii) blocking arm extended to same shoulder
    iii) palm facing direct toward you

c) double factors:
    i) not crossing to center line

© 2014 EPAKS Publications

Examples of bad outward Blocks
(improper width, angle, and shrugged shoulders)

Improving Your Execution of Long Form One

Upward Block

a) not obeying the rule of Margin for Error:
    i) done like chicken wings, no torque, just arm lifting

b) proper alignments:
    i) ending with angle of deflection (from overhead attack)
    ii) blocking arm extended to top of head
    iii) blocking arm extended to opposite shoulder
    iv) fist positioned (palm facing directly forward) forward at 45 degrees away from you

c) double factors:
    i) crossing past center line

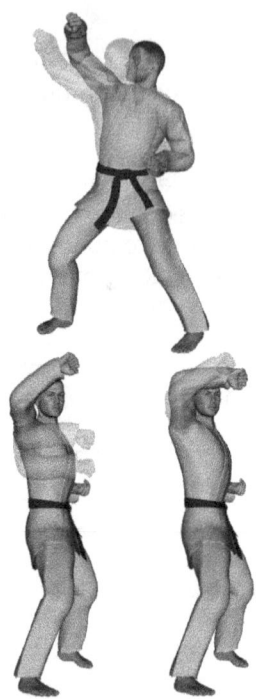

Examples of bad upward
Blocks
(leaning, improper transition,
and improper angle)

Downward Block

a) not obeying Economy of Motion principle:
   i) chamber motion done too high (face height instead parallel to ground)

b) proper alignments:
   i) blocking arm extended parallel to front knee after execution
   ii) blocking arm extended to same shoulder
   iii) palm facing directly downward
   iv) elbow slightly bent during and after execution of block (not "locked out")

c) double factors:
   iii) not executed with palm up (instead with palm down)

| 276 | The Official EPAKS Guide to Long Form One |

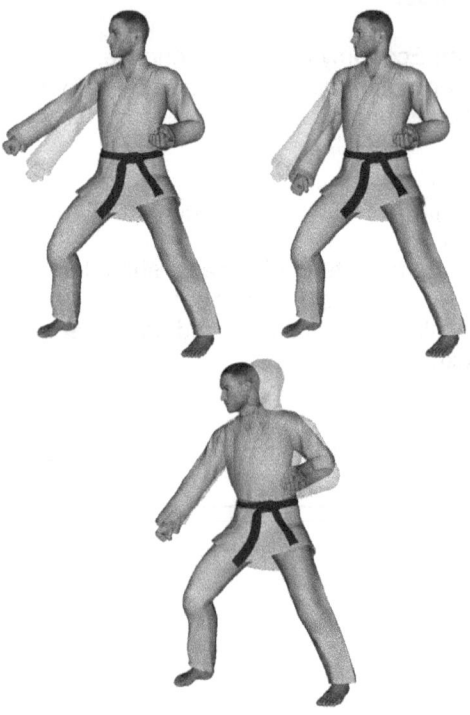

Examples of bad Downward Blocks
(improper height - high / low and leaning)

Inside Downward - Palm Up

a) not obeying Economy of Motion principle:
   i) chamber motion done too high (face height instead parallel to ground)

b) proper alignments:
   i) blocking arm extended parallel to front knee after execution (if in neutral bow)
   ii) blocking arm extended to center-line (not beyond)
   iii) palm facing directly upward

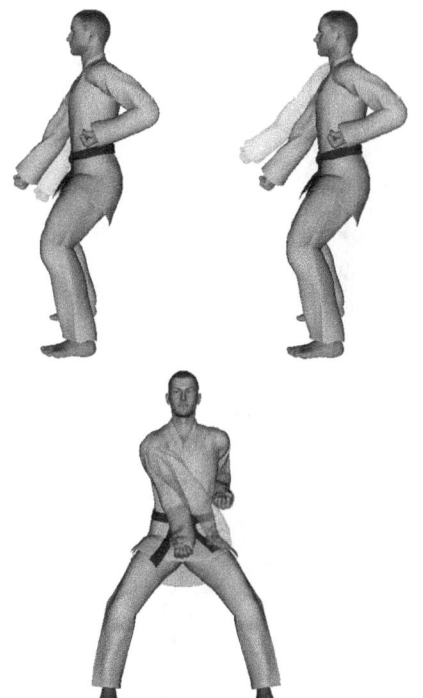

Examples of bad Inside-Downward, Palm Up Blocks
(improper height - high / low)
(Improper width - narrow)

Inside Downward - Palm Down

a) not obeying Economy of Motion principle:
   i) chamber motion done too high (dropped to outside of hip before execution)

b) proper alignments:
   i) blocking arm extended parallel to front knee after execution (if in neutral bow)
   ii) blocking arm extended to opposite shoulder
   iii) palm facing directly downward

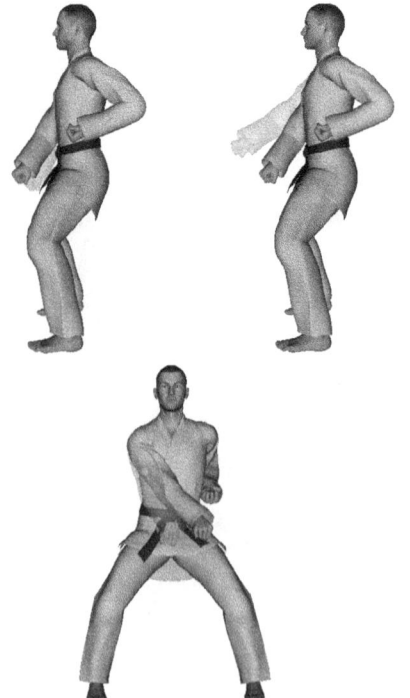

Examples of bad Inside-Downward, Palm Down Blocks
(improper height - high / low)
(Improper width - narrow)

Push-Down

a) not obeying Economy of Motion principle:
    i) chamber motion done too high (face height instead of sternum)

b) proper alignments:
    i) blocking hand extended parallel to front knee after execution (if in neutral bow)
    ii) blocking hand extended to groin height
    iii) fingers of blocking hand pointing backward at slight angle
    iv) fingers of blocking hand raised higher than heel-of-palm
    v) block executed down center-line

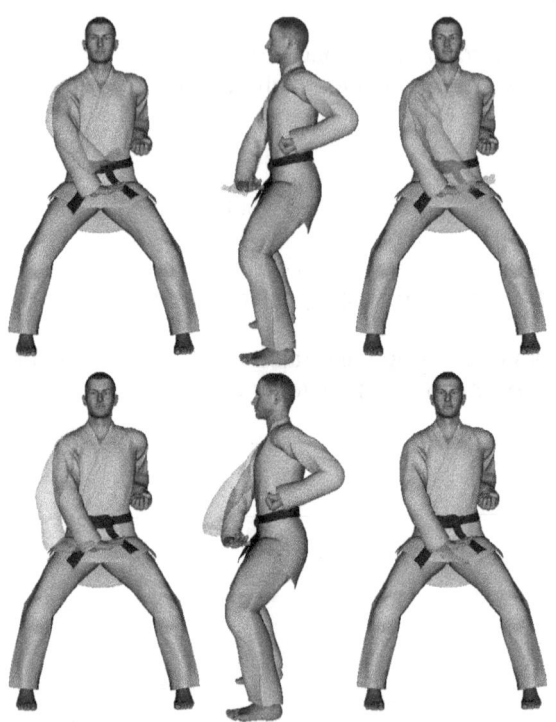

Examples of bad Push-Down Blocks
(improper height - high)
(improper rotation - fingers pointing outward)
(improper width - to left / to right)
(Improper depth - too far)
(improper rotation - finger pointing downward)

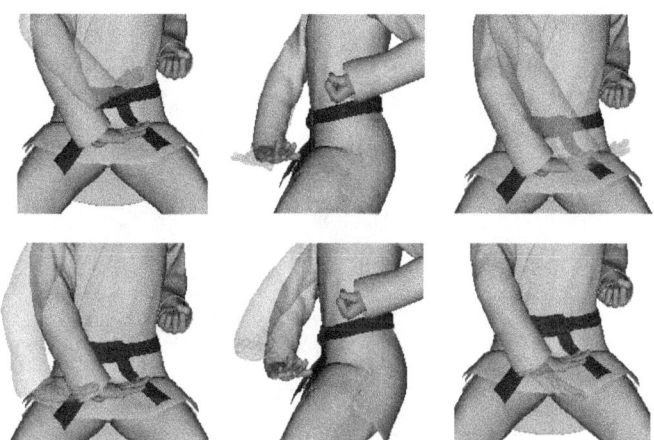

Examples of bad Push-Down Blocks
(Close-up of above examples)

Strikes

Strikes (offense) is one of the two major themes of Long Form One. Executing the strikes properly can make the difference between a successful offense and failure. Just like the stances and the blocks, the practitioner should become intimately familiar with the proper dimensions utilized in each of the strikes. Some of the primary concepts in dealing with striking are Angle of Incidence, Directional Harmony, Focus, Alignment, and Method of Execution. These theories along with others are highlighted in detail in SGM Parker's book, "Infinite Insights into Kenpo, book #3 (Physical Analyzation II)."

Some of the most common mistakes displayed while executing Long Form One strikes are: not executing the strikes to the proper dimensions; not executing the strikes to the proper angles; not extending the strike to the proper depth; not executing the strikes with the proper point of contact of the weapon; and/or executing the strike with improper timing.

Improving Your Execution of Long Form One   283

Strike Errors

a) not obeying Economy of Motion principle:
   i) not executing the strike from Point of Origin

b) improper alignments:
   i) executed to improper dimensions
   ii) executed with improper body alignments
   ii) incorrect Point of Contact of weapon with target (hitting with wrong part of weapon)

c) improper formation of weapon

d) improper execution:
   i) executed with wrong Method of Execution

e) not executing the strikes smoothly - i.e. mechanical / staccato motion

Straight Punch (including Isolation)

a) improper alignments:
    i) not executed at chest level
    ii) not extended to proper depth:
        1) punching arm not fully extended
        2) elbow hyper-extended
    iii) wrist bent improperly:
        1) not punching with the first two knuckles of fist (horizontal bend)
        2) wrist bent too much (vertical bend)
        3) wrist bent not enough (vertical bend)
    iv) improper stance (see Stance Errors section) (see examples below)
    v) improper rotation
        1) fist not rotated to be parallel with ground

b) improper formation of fist:
    i) thumb
        1) not wrapped over bottom of fingers (for standard punch)
        2) not pressed tightly again rest of fist (punch variation - aka "sun" fist)
        3) tucked under index finger
    ii) fingers
        1) not fully bent (aka not creating Compact Unit)
        2) not all finger bent properly

c) improper execution:
    i) executed with elbow not contouring own body (aka "chicken winging")
    ii) executed not directly to target (arching line of travel)
    iii) execution not at proper speeds / methods
        1) executed too slow (transforms into push with knuckles)
        2) executed too fast (body unable to keep up with strike)
        3) executed too tense (unable to achieve proper 'snap' of strike) (strike looks 'pushed' out)
        4) strike not tensed at Point of Contact (improper timing / never)

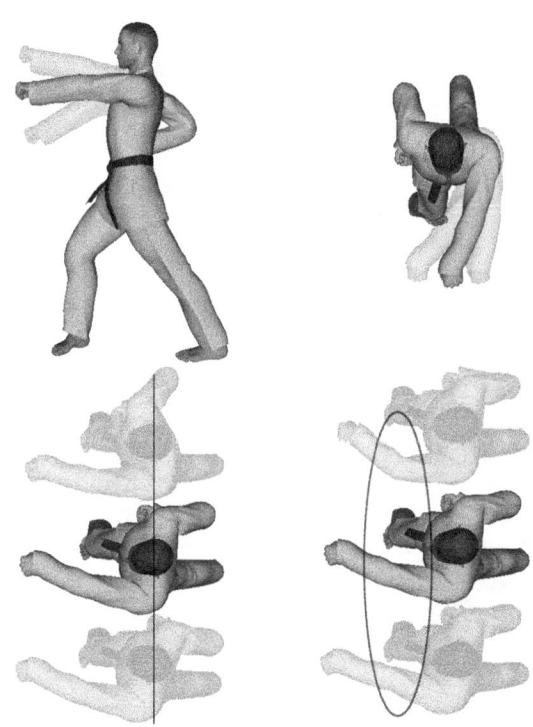

Examples of bad Straight Punches - dimensions
(improper height - high / low, width - not centered)
(improper rotation of stance - under / over, elbow extension - under / hyper)

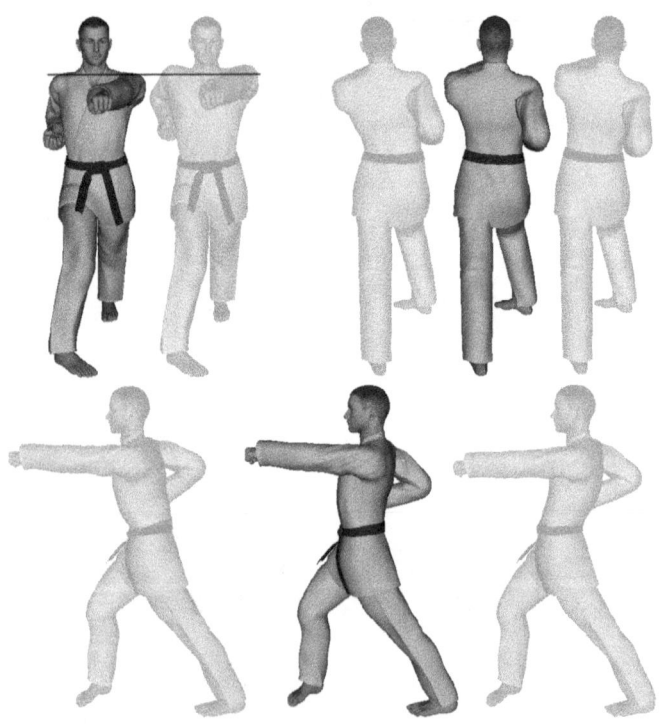

Examples of bad Straight Punch - positioning
(shrugged shoulders, leaning - side to side)
(leaning - forward / backward)

Improving Your Execution of Long Form One | 287

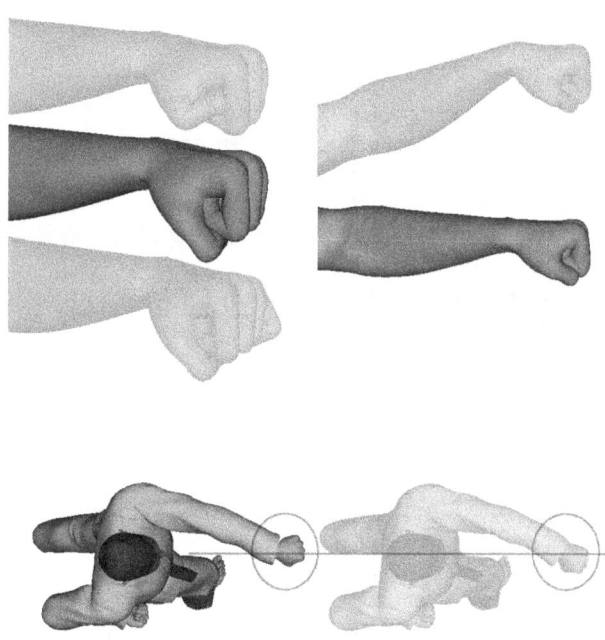

Examples of bad Straight Punch - weapon formation / angle
(formation - tucked thumb / hanging pinky finger)
(wrist: vertical angle - over bent)
(wrist: horizontal angle - contact with wrong knuckles)

Outward Elbow

a) improper alignments:
    i) not extended to proper depth:
        1) striking arm not fully extended
        2) striking arm over extended (forcing stance to lean toward Point of Reference)
    ii) fist not pointing directly downward
    iii) contact not made with tip of elbow (contact made with triceps muscle)
    iv) improper stance (see Stance Errors and Stance Errors - Fighting Horse sections)

b) improper formation of elbow:
    i) elbow not completely bent (not creating Compact Unit)

c) improper execution:
    i) not executed from Point of Origin of punch (where punch completed)
    ii) not executed on reverse line as punch
    iii) execution not at proper speeds / methods
        1) executed too slow (transforms into push with elbow)
        2) executed too fast (body unable to keep up with strike)
        3) executed too tense (unable to achieve proper 'snap' of strike) (strike looks 'pushed' out)
        4) strike not tensed at Point of Contact (improper timing / never)

Improving Your Execution of Long Form One

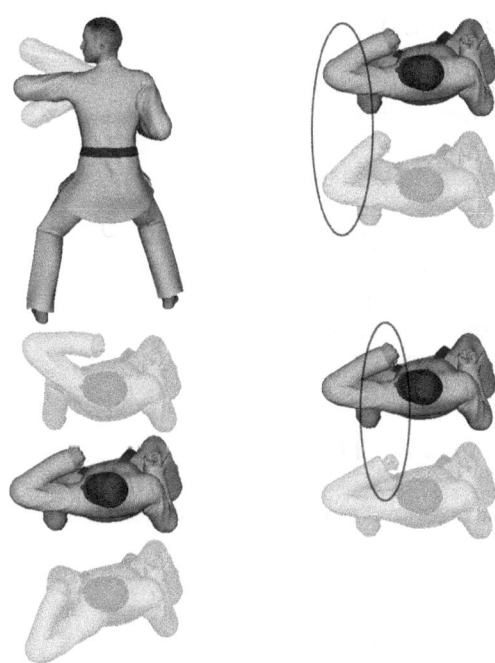

Examples of bad Elow
(Improper height, high / low)
(Improper bend - not compact)
(Improper rotation - under rotation / over rotation)
(Improper wrist rotation)

Isolation - Angled Punches

a) improper alignments:
    i) not executed at chest level
    ii) not extended to proper depth:
        1) punching arm not fully extended
        2) elbow hyper-extended
        3) over-extended to point of compromising horse stance
    iii) wrist bent improperly:
        1) not punching with the first two knuckles of fist (horizontal bend)
        2) wrist bent too much (vertical bend)
        3) wrist bent not enough (vertical bend)
    iv) improper stance (see Stance Errors section)

b) improper formation of fist:
    i) thumb
        1) not wrapped over bottom of fingers (for standard punch)
        2) not pressed tightly again rest of fist (punch variation - aka "sun" fist)
        3) tucked under index finger
    ii) fingers
        1) not fully bent (aka not creating Compact Unit)
        2) not all finger bent properly

c) improper execution:
    i) executed with elbow not contouring own body (aka "chicken winging")
    ii) execution not at proper speeds / methods
        1) executed too slow (transforms into push with knuckles)
        2) executed too fast (body unable to keep up with strike)
        3) executed too tense (unable to achieve proper 'snap' of strike) (strike looks 'pushed' out)
        4) strike not tensed at Point of Contact (improper timing / never)

d) improper gaze:

Improving Your Execution of Long Form One

i) not looking in direction of punches (optional)

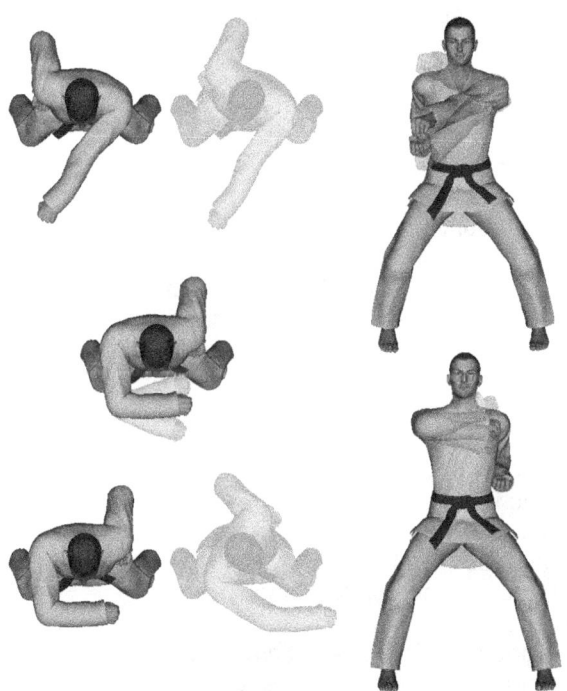

Examples of bad Angled Punches
(45 degree punch - over rotated)
(45 degree - punch too high / low)
(90 degree punch - too close / far)
(90 degree punch - over rotated)
(90 degree punch - too high / low)

Isolation - Uppercut Punch

a) improper alignments:
    i) not executed to solar plexus level
    ii) not extended to proper depth:
        1) punching arm not pointing upward at 45 degree angle
        2) elbow over-extended (should extend to just past ribs)
    iii) not executed to center-line
    iv) wrist bent improperly:
        1) not punching with the first two knuckles of fist (horizontal bend)
        2) wrist bent too much (vertical bend)
        3) wrist bent not enough (vertical bend)
    v) fist not fully inverted (palm pointing upward)

b) improper formation of fist:
    i) thumb
        1) not wrapped over bottom of fingers (for standard punch)
        2) not pressed tightly again rest of fist (punch variation - aka "sun" fist)
        3) tucked under index finger
    ii) fingers
        1) not fully bent (aka not creating Compact Unit)
        2) not all finger bent properly

c) improper execution:
    i) executed with elbow not contouring own body (aka "chicken winging")
    ii) execution not at proper speeds / methods
        1) executed too slow (transforms into push with knuckles)
        2) executed too fast (body unable to keep up with strike)
        3) executed too tense (unable to achieve proper 'snap' of strike) (strike looks 'pushed' out)
        4) strike not tensed at Point of Contact (improper timing / never)

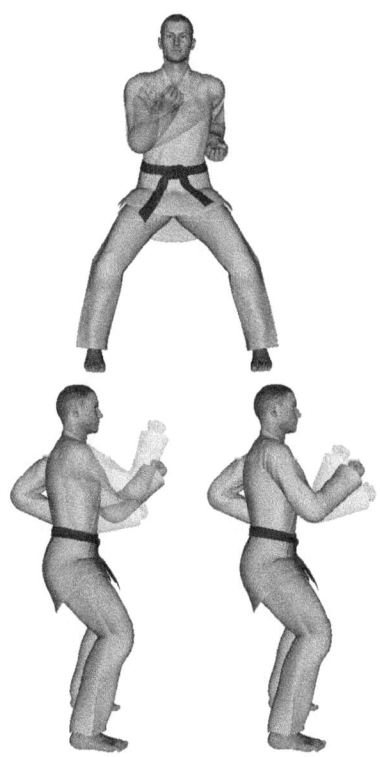

Examples of bad Upper-cut Punch
(improper width - too vertical / too horizontal)
(improper height - too high / too low)
(improper depth - elbow too bent / elbow not bent enough)

Improvement Priorities

The following chart is designed to help the practitioner correct the majority of errors illustrated in this chapter. It provides the practitioner with a chart that maps the commonality of errors against the severity of errors.

To start fixing errors in Long Form One, start with the errors in the upper right hand corner and work downward and to the left of the graph. This will ensure the most sever errors and common errors are fixed first.

It is not feasible to get all possible errors onto a chart such as this. Therefore, errors are often combined into an error category (such as Stance Dimensions) which contains more than one error. To get more specific information on errors that are contained within a specific category, see the details presented in the other sections of this chapter.

In general, one can also use the priority of the basics as a guide with which to use for correcting errors. These priorities are as follows: stances, blocks, strikes, timing, alignment / formation, other. One should notice that using the 'priority of basics' method does not always coincide with sequence laid out in the chart presented below.

Note: this chart should be used in conjunction with the chart presented in the same section of the "EPAKS Guide to Short Form One" book.

Improving Your Execution of Long Form One

```
^                  Improper Fist - Formation           Improper Stance - Dimensions
^                                                      Improper Block - Dimensions
More Severe        Improper Step into Horse            Improper Strike - Dimensions
                   Improper Cover Step
                                              Improper Step Thru - Height

                                                 Improper Punch / Body Alignment
                                    Over / Under Rotation Executing Blocks / Strikes
|                                     Improper Stance - Weight Distribution

                   Improper Elbow - Formation                  Leaning in Stance
                                              Improper Stance - Foot Directionality
Less Severe                                   Improper Punch / Stance Shift - Timing
                                         Isolation Punch - Stance Shifting
<<                                              Improper Method of Execution
                                              Isolation Punch - Alignments
                                Improper Breathing
                                                         Improper Gaze Direction
```

<< Less Common   -   More Common >>

Improvement Chart
(start corrections from the upper-right and move to the lower-left)

Chapter 9 - Frequently Asked Questions

This section highlights information and provides new insights to the information provided in other sections of this guide: presenting it in a question and answer format. One of the things the Q&A format allows for is illustrating the information from a different perspective. This perspective change can sometimes allow the reader to more quickly and firmly grasp this information. It also can combine information across multiple areas of the guide together. Thus, allowing the reader to understand connections that are not as obvious as in other formats.

What is the timing of Long Form One?

The timing of Long Form One is called one-in-one timing or sometimes referred to as single beat timing. What that means is that for every foot / body maneuver there is a single defense / offensive maneuver. Both Short Form One and Long Form One share this timing. Other forms do not necessarily share this timing sequence. For instance, the Two's have a two-in-one timing sequence.

Why is Long Form One NOT a 'defense only' form?

This is due to two reasons:

1) The definition of Kenpo forms states that one of the purposes of the forms is to show reverses and opposites and the opposite of defense is offense.

2) By definition Long Form One builds upon Short Form One. And as such, Long Form One builds upon the physical defenses demonstrated in Short Form One by adding new blocks. But, it also must build upon it conceptually and the obvious next conceptual step from defense is its opposite, offense.

Why is the first offensive move in Long Form One the straight punch?

There are a number of reasons for this:

First, since, by definition, Long Form One must build upon Short Form One both physically and conceptually, and the next logical step from defense is offense - Long Form One moves from defense only to defense and offense. And, one of the easiest offensive moves to deliver is the straight punch.

Second, since Long Form One is primarily a closed hand form, it makes sense that the offensive maneuvers be closed handed as well - and one of the easiest and most commonly used offensive maneuvers is the straight punch.

Third, since the first defense executed in Short Form One / Long Form One is the inward block, it makes logical sense to execute the offensive maneuver that the defense is typically used against - the straight punch.

Fourth, all Short Form One defenses are executed from the front hand while in a Neutral Bow. And, since Long Form One must build upon this sequence, it makes logical sense to group as many opposites and new information into a single maneuver as reasonably possible. This was done by executing the new offensive maneuver from of the rear hand, demonstrating the opposite side, along with demonstrating a new stance - the Forward Bow.

Fifth (continuing from Four), all Short Form One defenses are executed using a Path of Travel - the opposite of this concept is Line of Travel - which the straight punch demonstrates.

Sixth (continuing from Four), all Short Form One defenses are executed using the side (forearm) of the weapon - the opposite of this concept is to use the tip (knuckles) of the weapon - which the straight punch demonstrates.

© 2014 EPAKS Publications

| 300 | The Official EPAKS Guide to Long Form One |

Note: for further reading about more information presented from execution of this maneuver - see the Analysis of Long Form One section of this guide.

If American Kenpo is a strong sided system, why is the first punch a left?

This is due to the limitation of Long Form One expanding upon Short Form One. Since Short Form One's first maneuver is a right inward block, this limits the possibilities of the follow up maneuver. Since Long Form One is still a beginning form, path of travel for an offensive weapon needs to be emphasized. This leaves the rear (left) hand available to accomplish this goal.

What is the Primary Power Principle of the Straight Punch in Long Form One

The primary Power Principle of the Straight Punch is Torque. But, unlike the blocks there is also a secondary Power Principle - Back-up Mass.

The primary Power Principle is Torque because the majority of the power generated during the execution of the strike is through (direct) rotation - from the Neutral Bow to the Forward Bow. But, there is also an element of weight shift forward (from 50% - 50% to 60% - 40%). This weight shift adds an element of Back-up Mass.

Does the back foot settle with the block or the punch?

One of the most important rules in American Kenpo is to create a stable base. As such, a stable base must be in place before a block can be executed effectively - therefore, mandating that the back foot be settled by the anticipated point of contact of the block.

The ball of the foot is then used as the pivot point for shifting into the Forward Bow during the execution of the straight punch. In order to pivot on the ball of the foot into a Forward Bow, it is not necessary to lift the heel from the ground. It is only required that the weight be shifted from the heel to the ball during the transition. At the conclusion of the shift, weight can then again be equally distributed between the ball of the foot and the heel.

© 2014 EPAKS Publications

Why is there only one cat stance near the beginning of the form?

The cat stance serves a number of purposes:

First it introduces the concept of a call-out or highlighted move. This concept can be described as - a maneuver that stands out from other moves in a form for the purpose of calling attention to information that the move exposes in the form.

Second, it introduces the concept of "previews of things to come." This concept can be described as - a specific maneuver that introduces the practitioner to information that is not specifically detailed in the current form, but will be detailed in a future form. In this case, this maneuver previews the concept of an intersection - which is detailed in depth in Short Form Two.

Third, this maneuver highlights the Economy of Motion principle for Step Through reverse maneuvers. It forces the practitioner to anchor their rear (left) heel to the ground, thus illustrating that the Step Through reverse foot maneuver should be executed the same way. This is necessary because a common mistake for beginning practitioners is to "break their heel" while executing the Step Through reverse. "Breaking the heel" refers to lifting and sliding the heel to its new position prior to executing the Step Through reverse - rather than anchoring the heel to the floor and pivoting on the ball of the foot during the execution of the Step Through reverse. Executing the Step Through reverse and "breaking the heel" breaks the principle of Economy of Motion and should be corrected. For more information about correcting improper moves in Long Form One, see the "Improving Your Execution of Long Form One" section of this book.

Frequently Asked Questions 305

Fourth, this maneuver introduces the concept of "most everything you can do with your upper body, you can do with your lower body." This concept is fairly self explanatory and up to this maneuver only the upper body was used to maneuver into the intersection position - via double factoring blocks. With this maneuver both the lower and upper body are drawn into the intersection position, highlighting the above concept.

Finally, the above analysis is limited to only the information pertinent to this form and further analysis of this maneuver should be done by the reader to expose more information beyond this scope. In other words, there is more information that is contained in this simple maneuver, but is beyond the scope of just Long Form One analysis. The reader is encouraged to analyze this maneuver further utilizing the information that is presented in the higher forms.

Why are there triple blocks in the second half of Long Form One?

The triple blocks in Long Form One introduce defensive maneuvers using the rear hand. This is important because Short Form One is limited to defense with the front hand only. And, one opposite of this concept is defense using the rear hand.

Along with the triple blocks, there is also other information that is of interest within this section of the form. First, the left side of Short Form One is built into this section. This fact negates the requirement that Short Form One must be executed on both sides. Second, this section adds a whole new set of counter-rotational torques that are not present in Short Form One. Specifics of this information can be found through further analysis of this section of the form and in the Analysis of Long Form One section of this book.

Why do we step forward on the first downward block?

The step forward with the downward block serves a number of purposes:

First, it exposes another call-out or highlighted move. This concept can be described as - a maneuver that stands out from other moves in a form for the purpose of calling attention to information that the move exposes in the form.

Second, it exposes another "preview of things to come." This concept can be described as - a specific maneuver that introduces the practitioner to information that is not specifically detailed in the current form, but will be detailed in a future form. In this case, this maneuver previews the concept of advancing (going forward) - which is detailed in depth in Short and Long Form Two.

Finally, the above analysis is limited to only the information pertinent in this form and further analysis of this maneuver should be done by the reader to expose more information beyond this scope. In other words, there is more information that is contained in this simple maneuver, but is beyond the scope of just Long Form One analysis. The reader is encouraged to analyze this maneuver further utilizing the information that is presented in the higher forms.

© 2014 EPAKS Publications

Why is there no forward bow when executing the triple blocks?

Not shifting to the forward bow while executing the blocks from the rear arm serves a number of purposes:

First, not shifting completely to the forward isolates the upper body from the lower body, which simulates a sitting position. By doing this, the practitioner is exposed to the situation where defense while sitting may be necessary. This explanation is what is typically taught to the beginning practitioner who asks this question. But, as the readers of this book are aware, American Kenpo forms are not prearranged fighting situations - they define and show motion (see the "Understanding American Kenpo Forms" section of this book a for more detailed explanation).

Second, not shifting completely to the forward bow introduces the concept of "degrees of." This concept can be thought of as a spectrum containing all of the possible "degrees of" what is being represented. In this case rotation to the forward bow. Full rotation to the forward bow is achieved by execution of the punches in the first part of the form. Therefore, it is imperative that somewhere in the forms partial rotation into the forward bow must be demonstrated - i.e. a "degree of" rotation into the forward bow. This is demonstrated with the triple blocks, by not rotating the lower half of the body with the upper half of the body. Thus helping to obey the definition of an American Kenpo form.

© 2014 EPAKS Publications

What are 'isolations' and why are they important?

Isolation moves are another form of call-out or highlighted maneuvers. They are designed to visually and physically isolate specific maneuvers such that they stand out in a form. The purpose of this is to draw attention to the maneuvers, so that the initiated practitioner is subtly directed to analyze these maneuvers further for the purpose of exposing their true meaning in the form.

An isolation maneuver shows one or more of the following:
    i) previews of things to come
    ii) new information
    iii) missing information

From this, the practitioner can filter their analysis of the isolation maneuvers to more quickly determine there true meaning in the form.

What part of our fist do we punch with in Long Form One?

All punches, by definition, make contact with the front of the first two knuckles of the fist. If contact is made with other parts of the hand or knuckles, then the maneuver is no longer defined as a punch - rather it falls into the broader term, strike.

For instance, an outward back-knuckle is not a punch, it is a strike. This is because the contact point on the fist is the back of the first two knuckles - thus giving the strike it's name.

What type of Elbow is Executed in Long Form One?

The elbow strike in Long Form One is an Outward Elbow. Even though the strike is initiated from a reverse bow, the transition into the fighting horse defines the strike as outward. If the reverse bow was maintained, the elbow would have been a back elbow strike.

As a side note: If the reverse bow was maintained and the strike was delivered as a back elbow, the fist would have to be rotated completely upward (toward 12:00V) to be executed correctly - instead of only half way (facing you), as it is done in the form.

How does Long Form One relate to Short Form One?

In simple terms Long Form One builds upon Short Form One. By this one can correctly conclude that Long Form One contains all of the information presented in Short Form One an more. For a more complete explanation of this see the "Understanding Long Form One" section of this book.

What is the difference between Thrusting and Hammering Methods of Execution?

Thrusting and Hammering are only two of the Methods of Execution of strikes and blocks. There names basically describe what they are. More specifically:

Thrusting is a move delivered from a specific Point of Origin. That specific Point of Origin is where ever the weapon is positioned at the time of delivery. In most cases, from a chambered position or from a natural hanging position. This correctly implies that thrusting maneuvers typically are delivered in an upward direction. Thrusting also correctly implies that the weapon is not cocked - i.e. brought to an optimal position before being delivered.

Hammering is a move delivered from a cocked position. Cocking correctly implies optimal positioning of the weapon prior to delivery. Typically this is a position higher than the intended point of contact. This correctly implies that hammering maneuvers typically are delivered in a downward direction. Hammering gets its name from the similarity to hammering a nail with a hammer.

So what's the difference? Thrusting is, by definition, almost always faster than Hammering - because the weapon is delivered from where ever it is positioned prior to delivery. Contrast that with Hammering, which must be cocked to an optimal position prior to delivery - thus, creating more delivery time. But, by definition, Hammering is almost always stronger than Thrusting. This is for the same reason - the weapon is cocked to the optimal position prior to delivery, allowing for a stronger delivery.

To get a further explanation, research the American Kenpo terms - Phonetics of Motion, By the Numbers; and Word, Sentence, Paragraph of Motion. They can be found in SGM Parker's books: Infinite Insights into Kenpo series and Encyclopedia of Kenpo.

© 2014 EPAKS Publications

What is the difference between an opposite and a reverse?

In general terms, reverse is typically limited to motion staying on the same line, plane, or circle - but in directly opposing directions. Opposite is the broader of the two terms and is usually used in conceptual as well as physical contexts. Yet the terms are often used interchangeably - even though there are subtle differences between the two.

Also, opposite can be thought of as the umbrella term covering both opposite and reverse. While reverse is typically limited to directly opposing motions. Therefore one can correctly say - all reverses are opposites, but not all opposites are reverses.

To see a more complete answer of this question see Appendix C of this book.

Why shouldn't we visualize an opponent while executing this form?

Visualizing an opponent is a good mental exercise for learning how to focus a maneuver to a specific point in space. By visualizing, one can pretend to be blocking an incoming attack, giving the blocks more urgency and focus. But, as in all American Kenpo forms, there is no intention for there to be an imaginary opponent. Rather, that the form demonstrates: the rules and principles of motion, that everything has a reverse and an opposite, and gives and example. Visualizing an opponent can detract from this goal and lead the practitioner into treating the form as a preordained imaginary fight, rather than a demonstration of motion study and analysis.

If this form is for someone just starting, a beginner, why does it have so much information?

All American Kenpo forms contain an abundance of information. This is due to the fact that all American Kenpo forms, by definition, are designed to demonstrate information present in the system - and are not preordained, imaginary fights. But, as in all information contained in American Kenpo, it is designed to be absorbed over a long period of time. For example, a beginning student might not be expected to understand the different types of torque displayed in Long Form One. But, the beginner would most likely be expected to understand a lot of the opposite information contained in the form. But, as the practitioner continues to progress in American Kenpo, this information would be expected to be learned and absorbed at some point in their training.

Because of this layering of information, in American Kenpo, it is not only important to be able to execute the form properly; but as the practitioner becomes more and more advanced, it is expected that they also begin to understand more and more about the information presented in each form. And, that the practitioner also be able to explain this information in ever increasing detail, upon request.

If I'm not visualizing an imaginary opponent, where and what should I look at when doing the form?

When executing Long Form One, the practitioner should keep their gaze at eye level and parallel to the floor at all times.

How does leaning affect me?

Leaning can be done in a number of ways. First, one can just lean while settled in a stance (leaning); or, one can lean while maneuvering between stances (jet lagging). Either way, the back is not kept perpendicular to the ground.

In the case of a settled Neutral Bow stance, leaning can decrease both the stability of a stance and decrease maneuverability of the stance. A straight back places the weight and position of the body in the center of the stance, i.e. the Intersection Position. From the Intersection Position it is more efficient to go in any possible direction. Also, when leaning it is easier for the attacker to make the defender go in one direction over another, because the defender's body is already positioned favoring a direction, which can be exploited.

In the case of maneuvering between stances, leaning creates precession. Precession is the wobble of a rotation that is not perfectly aligned vertically with its axis. For example the earth has a precession in its rotation. A precession, in this case, creates inefficiencies in rotation, breaking the principle of Economy of Motion. Also, leaning can create Jet Lagging. Jet Lagging is created by allowing the head and upper body to follow the lower body (instead of with the lower body) while stepping through in reverse. Since the purpose of stepping away is to create distance, letting the upper body lag behind the lower body exposes the face to the opponent for a longer period of time than necessary – creating a defensive problem, which can be exploited by the opponent.

Why is the form done in the "+" instead of another pattern?

The plus '+' pattern is the most simplistic pattern presented in American Kenpo forms. It contains the most basic opposite elements: front - back and left - right. Put together, these opposites form the plus '+' pattern. Also, this pattern lays out the two (2) major lines and the four (4) major angles for American Kenpo: 12:00 - 6:00 line and 9:00 - 3:00 line. Later forms begin to use the remaining minor lines: 10:30 - 4:30 line and 1:30 - 7:30 line.

Did SGM Parker create Long Form One?

Yes. For further information about the history of Long Form One read the "History of Long Form One" section of this book.

What is meant by a 'dictionary' form?

Dictionary forms (i.e. Short Form One, Long Form One, Short Form Two, Long Form Two) concentrate more on 'defining' motion over theories and concepts. The 'encyclopedia' forms (i.e. the higher forms), rely more heavily on theories and concepts. While the 'appendix' forms (i.e. the sets) rely on concentrated information about a subject (i.e. kicking, blocking, finger strikes, etc.).

Chapter 10 - Quizzes

This section contains quizzes that can be used to test one's understanding of Long Form One. They are designed to be used by the reader themselves, or by an instructor to query a student's understanding of the information presented in Long Form One. There are two groups of tests presented: 1) beginner to intermediate and 2) advanced. And, each group is broken down into two types of tests: 1) multiple choice and 2) fill in the blank.

The answers to each of the quizzes can be found in Appendix A at the back of this guide.

Multiple Choice - Beginner / Intermediate

1) The right hammering inward block of Long Form One differs from Short Form One:
   a) its held longer
   b) its executed harder
   c) the timing is different
   d) all of the above
   e) none of these

2) Long Forms do what to Short Forms:
   a) extend
   b) ignore
   c) simplify
   d) all of the above
   e) none of these

3) what information is shared between Short Form One and Long Form One:
   a) defense with front hand
   b) neutral bow
   c) retreating
   d) all of the above
   e) none of these

4) new information introduced in Long Form One that is not in Short Form One:
   a) new stances
   b) new blocks
   c) advancing
   d) all of the above
   e) none of these

© 2014 EPAKS Publications

5) in what direction should the punches be executed at in the isolation of Long Form One?
   a) straight ahead
   b) to the side
   c) angled upward
   d) all of the above
   e) none of these

6) what part of the fist should make contact while punching in Long Form One:
   a) the back of the hand
   b) all the knuckles
   c) front of the outer knuckles
   d) depends upon what is being hit
   e) front of the first two knuckles

7) the elbow in Long Form One is done:
   a) with the left arm
   b) with the right arm
   c) there is no elbow
   d) before the outward block
   e) in the isolation

8) the block sequence of the isolation in Long Form One is:
   a) inside-downward palm up/push-down/inside downward palm down
   b) inside-downward palm down/inside-downward palm up/push-down
   c) push-down/inside-downward palm down/inside downward palm up
   d) inside-downward palm up/inside-downward palm down/push-down
   e) none of these

9) what is the block sequence of the triple block section of Long Form One:
   a) down / up / out / in
   b) in / out / down / up
   c) out / in / up / down
   d) up / down / in / out
   e) none of these

10) how many cat stances are there in Long Form One:
    a) 1
    b) 2
    c) 3
    d) 8
    e) none

11) the advantages of a forward bow are:
    a) better bracing angle
    b) better front to back stability
    c) more reach with the rear hand
    d) all of the above
    e) none of these

12) the foot rotation (positioning) on a forward bow is:
    a) both feet facing sideways
    b) both feet facing forward
    c) the front foot facing forward diagonally / the rear foot facing forward
    d) the front foot facing sideways / the rear foot facing forward

13) the weight distribution of a forward bow is:
   a) 40-60
   b) 50-50
   c) 60-40
   d) 30-70
   e) 100%

---

14) Long Form One introduces how many types of new blocks:
   a) 1
   b) 2
   c) 3
   d) 4
   e) none

---

15) Long Form One introduces:
   a) the forward bow stance
   b) the cat stance
   c) offensive moves
   d) all of the above
   e) none of these

---

16) the pattern of lf1 is:
   a) "L"
   b) "x"
   c) "+"
   d) "T"
   e) "H"

---

17) all punches of Long Form One:
    a) are strikes
    b) are executed on a line of travel
    c) make contact with the knuckles
    d) all of the above
    e) none of these

18) when shifting to a forward bow in Long Form One, always shift:
    a) the front foot
    b) the back foot
    c) both feet
    d) neither of the feet
    e) on the heel of either foot

19) the opposite direction of all the downward blocks are:
    a) the upward blocks
    b) the push down blocks
    c) the vertical outward blocks
    d) all of the above
    e) none of the above

20) the isolation in Long Form One shows:
    a) previews of things to come
    b) new information
    c) missing information
    d) all of the above
    e) none of these

21) the opposite of the right inward block is:
   a) a left inward block
   b) a right straight punch
   c) a right outward block
   d) all of the above
   e) none of these

22) the isolation moves in Long Form One are done from a:
   a) horse stance
   b) neutral bow
   c) forward bow
   d) all of the above
   e) none of these

23) when is the first time we step forward in Long Form One:
   a) on the first upward block
   b) on the last downward block
   c) on the first punch
   d) like Short Form One, this form only retreats
   e) none of the above

24) information introduced in Long Form One that was not in Short Form One:
   a) isolation
   b) offense
   c) the use of the rear hand
   d) all of the above
   e) none of these

25) the 'theme' stance of Long Form One is the:
   a) cat stance
   b) neutral bow
   c) reverse bow
   d) horse stance
   e) forward bow

Fill in the Blank - Beginner / Intermediate

1) Punches are delivered on a _____ of travel
   _____

2) The forward bow in Long Form One is used to deliver a _____
   _____

3) The _____ side of Short Form One is shown with the triple block section of Long Form One
   _____

4) The forward bow in Long Form One shows a _____ angle
   _____

5) The right _____ cat stance is highlighted in Long Form One
   _____

6) There are _____ punches in the isolation of Long Form One
   _____

7) Punches always make contact with the _____ of the first two knuckles
   _____

8) There are _____ outward blocks in Long Form One
   _____

9) There are _____ upward blocks in Long Form One (excluding double-factors)
   _____

10) The triple blocks introduce blocking with the _____ hand

11) The inside-downward palm up block is delivered with a _____ Method of Execution

12) The inside-downward palm down block is delivered with a _____ Method of Execution

13) The punches in Long Form One are delivered with a _____ Method of Execution

14) There are(is) _____ isolation(s) section(s) in Long Form One

15) The first punch of the isolation is done with the _____ arm

16) There are _____ moves in the standard execution of Long Form One

17) The shared stance between Short Form One and Long Form One is the _____ bow

18) The first right punch is delivered toward _____

19) Long Form One teaches you to pivot on the _____ of your foot

20) Adjusting your foot prior to a foot maneuver is commonly referred to as _____ your heel

21) The reverse block to the inside-downward palm down is the _____ block

22) The only block in Long Form One that is not designed to make contact with your forearm is the _____ block

23) You should not hold your _____ during the execution of Long Form One

24) Long Form One faces _____ directions

25) Stances are designed to create a stable _____ in Long Form One

© 2014 EPAKS Publications

Multiple Choice - Advanced

1) the elbow in Long Form One is executed:
   a) palm up
   b) palm facing you
   c) palm facing away from you
   d) palm down
   e) does not matter

2) How does the first downward block of Long Form One differ from Short Form One:
   a) it is done advancing
   b) it is done from a different point of origin
   c) it is done beginning from a different stance
   d) all of the above
   e) none of these

3) Long Form One:
   a) starts the dictionary forms
   b) ends the dictionary forms
   c) is not part of the dictionary forms
   d) is an appendix form
   e) none of these

4) the opposite of defense is:
   a) a punch
   b) an elbow
   c) offense
   d) all of the above
   e) none of these

© 2014 EPAKS Publications

5) the first upward block sequence in Long Form One differs from Short Form One:
   a) the first block is done with a different power principle
   b) the third block is done from a new position
   c) in Long Form One it begins with a 180 degree cover
   d) all of the above
   e) none of these

6) information shared between Short Form One and Long Form One:
   a) three different types of torque
   b) methods of execution
   c) stance alignments
   d) all of the above
   e) none of these

7) the hidden stomp after the cat stance in Long Form One shows:
   a) settling
   b) weight transfer
   c) body harmony
   d) the opposite side to the stomp in the isolation
   e) there is no stomp

8) there are how many types of punches in Long Form One:
   a) 1
   b) 2
   c) 5
   d) 6
   e) 8

9) information introduced in Long Form One that is not in Short Form One:
   a) line of travel
   b) defense with the rear hand
   c) intersection position
   d) all of the above
   e) none of these

10) each block / punch sequence in the beginning half of Long Form One is always:
    a) executed to a different direction
    b) executed with the same Method of Execution
    c) executed utilizing all three Power Principles
    d) all of the above
    e) none of these

11) how many points of contact with your body would you make with an imaginary opponent in Long Form One: (hint - include both left and right sides)
    a) 1
    b) 3
    c) 5
    d) 9
    e) 13

12) the advantages of a forward bow are:
    a) increases gravitational marriage
    b) maximizes defense from straight ahead (12:00H)
    c) increases weapon availability
    d) all of the above
    e) none of these

© 2014 EPAKS Publications

13) the opposite of offense is:
   a) blocking
   b) defense
   c) covering
   d) all of the above
   e) none of these

---

14) Long Form One demonstrates how many offensive ranges of contact:
   a) 1
   b) 2
   c) 3
   d) 4
   e) none

---

15) Long Form One introduces how many types of new punches:
   a) 1
   b) 2
   c) 3
   d) 4
   e) none

---

16) Long Form One introduces how many new types of formal stances:
   (hint - exclude hybrid stances)
   a) None
   b) 1
   c) 2
   d) 3
   e) 4

© 2014 EPAKS Publications

17) the foot pattern of Long Form One is:
   a) "T"
   b) "X"
   c) "L"
   d) "U"
   e) "Y"

---

18) the first counter-rotational torque move in Long Form One is:
   a) the first left punch
   b) the second downward block
   c) the second outward block
   d) the first set of triple blocks
   e) the back elbow

---

19) the push-downs in Long Form One show:
   a) new point of contact for block
   b) open handed blocking
   c) preview of things to come for Short Form Two
   d) all of the above
   e) none of the above

---

20) how many types of downward blocks are in Long Form One:
   a) 1
   b) 2
   c) 4
   d) 8
   e) 17

© 2014 EPAKS Publications

21) the right arm is retracted to match the right 45 degree cat 'highlighted' stance:
    a) to cover the center line
    b) to show what we can do with our arms we can do with our legs
    c) to introduce framing
    d) all of the above
    e) none of the above

22) we don't shift into the forward bow with the triple blocks because:
    a) to maintain line of sight for our blocks
    b) to maximize counter-rotational torque
    c) to get total body harmony
    d) all of the above
    e) none of the above

23) the punches in the isolation show:
    a) the 'x' lines
    b) the category completion of the punches
    c) new methods of execution
    d) all of the above
    e) none of the above

24) The reverse of the upper-cut punches in Long Form One are:
    a) the straight punches
    b) the back elbow
    c) the push-downs
    d) all of the above
    e) none of the above

25) how many times do we step toward the front in Long Form One:
    a) 2
    b) 3
    c) 4
    d) 8
    e) none

Fill in the Blank - Advanced

1) The elbow is the _____ of the straight punch in Long Form One

2) The shift into the forward bow with the punch should be done _____

3) Long Form One contains the _____ side of Short Form One

4) The cat stance in Long Form One shows the _____ position

5) The first time we open our hands in a form is executing the _____

6) There are(is) _____ power principle(s) demonstrated in Long Form One

7) The only major direction missing from the isolation in Long Form One is _____

8) The triple blocks in Long Form One show how to _____ the upper body from the lower body

9) The elbow in Long Form One reverses the _____ of the punch

10) The inside-downward palm down block is the _____ of the downward block

11) The inside-downward palm down block is the _____ of the inside-downward palm up block

12) The strikes of Long Form One are executed with an angle of _____

13) There are _____ individual isolation movements in Long Form One

14) The blocks of Long Form One are demonstrated to all _____ height zones

15) Double factor blocks typically pass through the _____ position

16) There are _____ types of torque demonstrated in Long Form One

17) Long form One shows _____ types of hammering blocks

© 2014 EPAKS Publications

18) The _____ blocks show both hammering and thrusting Method of Execution

19) Double factor blocks fill the _____(s) in timing

20) Long Form One works on _____ in one timing

21) The primary difference between a step through and a cover in Long Form One is _____

22) Push-down blocks demonstrate how to block with the _____ of the weapon

23) The purpose of the outer rim concept in Long Form One is to eliminate _____ motion

24) Of the three types of forms in American Kenpo, Long Form One is classified as a(n) _____ form

25) The _____ block is the double factor block for upper height zone

Appendix 1 - Quiz Answers

These are the answers to the quizzes presented earlier in the guide. The answer section order matches the quiz section order presented earlier.

Multiple Choice Answers - Beginner / Intermediate

1) b
2) a
3) d
4) d
5) d
6) e
7) a
8) d
9) b
10) a
11) d
12) c
13) c
14) c
15) d
16) c
17) d
18) b
19) a
20) d
21) d
22) a
23) e
24) d
25) e

Fill in the Blank Answers - Beginner / Intermediate

1) line
2) punch
3) left
4) brace
5) 45 degree
6) eight
7) front
8) eight (8)
9) eight (8)
10) rear
11) hammering
12) thrusting
13) thrusting
14) one (1)
15) right
16) sixty (60)
17) neutral
18) 12:00
19) ball
20) breaking
21) downward
22) push-down
23) breath
24) four (4)
25) base

Multiple Choice Answers - Advanced

1) d
2) d
3) e
4) d
5) e
6) d
7) e
8) b
9) d
10) e
11) d
12) d
13) d
14) b
15) b
16) d
17) a
18) c
19) d
20) c
21) d
22) e
23) a
24) c
25) a

Fill in the Blank Answers - Advanced

1) reverse
2) simultaneously
3) opposite
4) intersection
5) push-downs
6) one (1)
7) backward
8) isolate
9) direction
10) reverse
11) opposite
12) incidence
13) sixteen (16)
14) three (3)
15) intersection
16) two (2)
17) two (2)
18) inward
19) gap
20) one (1)
21) direction
22) tip (or end)
23) wasted
24) dictionary
25) inward

Appendix 2 - The Kenpo Kards

The Kenpo Kards is a project by EPAKS that presents all of the American Kenpo self-defense techniques, forms, and sets to a quick reference card, which can be used for study and entertainment. The Kenpo Kards were released in three (3) decks - beginner, intermediate, and advanced. Along with the Kards, EPAKS produced a guide book to help in the usage of both the kards and understanding of some of the foundational layout of American Kenpo.

Along with the physical version of the kards and guide book, EPAKS has released a digital version of each. The Kenpo Kards app is available in both the Google Play store and the Amazon App store. The digital guide book is available in the Google Play store, the Amazon digital book store, and the Barnes and Noble digital book store.

© 2014 EPAKS Publications

The Kenpo Kard app allows the user to quickly sort and / or choose kards to study, and allows for user to play back the list for practicing alone or with up to five (5) partners. The app has options to select the speed to play back the list, choose which yellow belt techniques to use in the sorting (old / new / both), and select the highest technique one has learned. This app is invaluable in helping to understand relations between techniques, and quickly grouping techniques by similarities - such as same attack, same side forward, same web of knowledge grouping, just to name a few.

One of the most important things the reader should be aware of is that it is not the intent of the Kenpo Kards project to teach the practitioner how to do American Kenpo. But, rather to help the practitioner in understanding and exploring the information contained in what they have learned from their instructor.

© 2014 EPAKS Publications

The Front of the Kard

© 2014 EPAKS Publications

The first thing one will notice about the front of the kard is the signification of Long Form One. It is the most prominent image on the kard. This layout is part of a theme that is shared among all of the kards in the form dek. As the form increases in complexity, the signification becomes less prominent, while at the same time the figures on the kard become more prominent.

The next thing one should notice is that the figure on the kard is executing the first offensive move of Long Form One. This is part of another theme that shared among all the kards in the forms dek. The figure and any other images (aside from the signification) will highlight the most important pieces of information and / or physical attributes of the form being illustrated. It is the intent that a person familiar with the form should be able to quickly ascertain which form is being illustrated without having to read the text.

The Back of the Kard

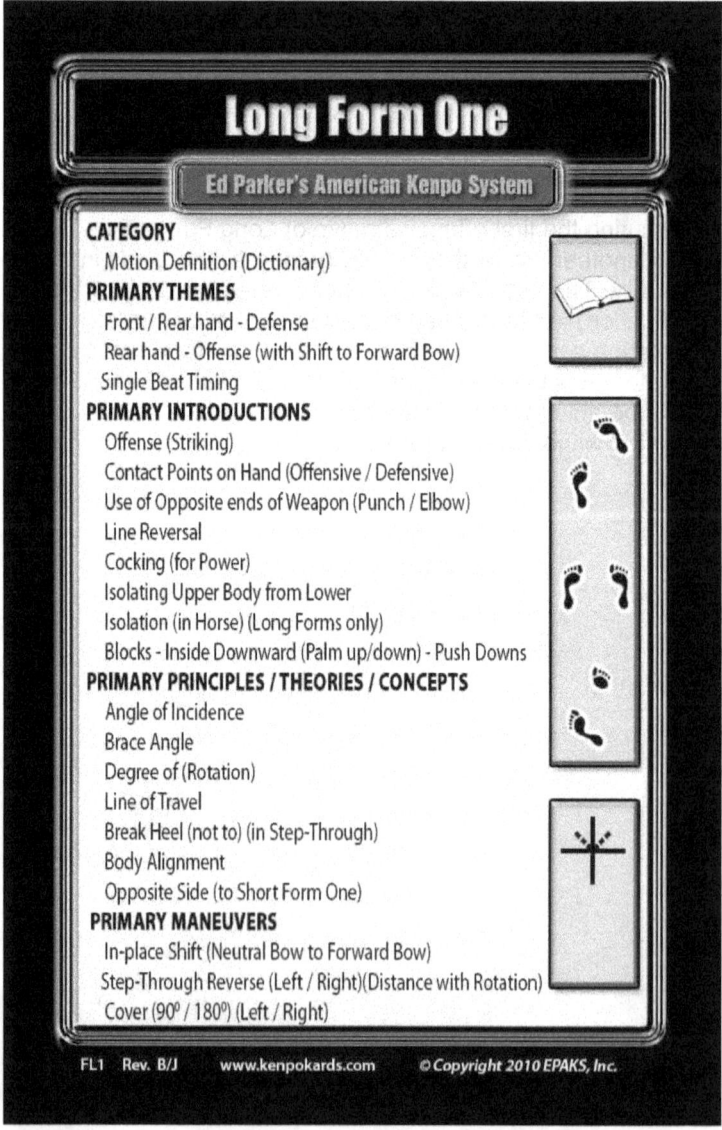

Long Form One
Ed Parker's American Kenpo System

CATEGORY
  Motion Definition (Dictionary)
PRIMARY THEMES
  Front / Rear hand - Defense
  Rear hand - Offense (with Shift to Forward Bow)
  Single Beat Timing
PRIMARY INTRODUCTIONS
  Offense (Striking)
  Contact Points on Hand (Offensive / Defensive)
  Use of Opposite ends of Weapon (Punch / Elbow)
  Line Reversal
  Cocking (for Power)
  Isolating Upper Body from Lower
  Isolation (in Horse) (Long Forms only)
  Blocks - Inside Downward (Palm up/down) - Push Downs
PRIMARY PRINCIPLES / THEORIES / CONCEPTS
  Angle of Incidence
  Brace Angle
  Degree of (Rotation)
  Line of Travel
  Break Heel (not to) (in Step-Through)
  Body Alignment
  Opposite Side (to Short Form One)
PRIMARY MANEUVERS
  In-place Shift (Neutral Bow to Forward Bow)
  Step-Through Reverse (Left / Right)(Distance with Rotation)
  Cover (90° / 180°) (Left / Right)

FL1   Rev. B/J   www.kenpokards.com   © Copyright 2010 EPAKS, Inc.

The Kenpo Kards 353

The back of the kard can quickly be described as a microcosm of this guide book. If you have read the book up to this point, the information presented on the kard should be very easy to understand without much further explanation. What follows is a breakdown of the design and intent of the kard.

The back of the kard can be divided up into two columns. The left column is a textual summary of the major information presented in Long Form One. The right column is a quick overview of other attributes about Long Form One, that are best or more quickly illustrated through images.

The Left Column

The left column lays out a quick overview of the major information presented in Long Form One. It should be noted that due to space limitations, not all information about Long Form One can be presented. So, a wide variety of the most important information has been included.

The left column is broken down into different 'categories of information.' This design is intended to help the practitioner in absorbing and comprehending the information in a more concentrated and targeted manner. In this way, the practitioner can be presented with related information, illustrated in a concise manner. Allowing the practitioner to quickly overview a lot of information in a short period of time.

As stated earlier, the information illustrated on the back of the kard is also presented in this guide book - but in a more descriptive manner. It is suggested that the reader use this guide book to help in researching further the information with which the reader is unfamiliar or needs to get more clarification on the details of this information.

© 2014 EPAKS Publications

The Right Column

The right column has three (3) rows.

1) The top row illustrates what category of form Long Form One falls into - in this case Dictionary (see Dictionary / Encyclopedia / Appendix analogy earlier in this book).

2) The middle row illustrates the theme stance of the form - in this case the Forward Bow. It also illustrates the new stances demonstrated in the form - in this case the horse stance and the cat stance.

3) The bottom row lays out the important patterns of Long Form One - in this case the directions of the punch isolation pattern at the end of the form.

Appendix 3 - Reverse and Opposite

Reverse and opposite are words we commonly use in not only the English language but also our American Kenpo language. But most people take these two words for granted and don't really think about the two words, what they mean, and what is the difference between the two. The purpose of this section is to clarify these two words in the reader's mind.

First let's start with the definitions of these two words. We will limit the definitions to definitions that are directly related to self-defense and specifically American Kenpo.

Opposite

1) To go in a completely contrary position, direction, order, sequence, timing, etc... - as in movement.
2) Completely contrary or opposing - as in definition, strategy, idea, concept, theory, or principle.
3) The back side of anything.

Reverse

1) To go in the opposite position, direction, order, sequence, timing, etc... - as in movement.
2) Completely contrary or opposing - as in definition, strategy, idea, concept, theory, or principle.
3) The back side of anything.

The first thing one should notice is that the only difference between these definitions is #1. #2 and #3 are exactly the

© 2014 EPAKS Publications

same. And, the #1 definitions are pretty close to one another. The major difference being the words "completely contrary" and "opposite." From this we can deduce that the terms reverse and opposite are generally very similar and can be, and often are, used interchangeably - but differ in subtle ways, depending upon the context in which each is used. As implied in the definitions, these terms, like a lot of terms, have both a physical and mental aspect to them.

In regards to physical motion - opposite and reverse at times can be used interchangeably as long as the physical motion stays on the same line, plane, or circle. Once deviation from a common line, plane, or circle occurs, opposite may still hold true, but reverse is no longer applicable. A good example of this is the concept of Reverse Motion vs Return Motion.

In regards to conceptual matters - one typically refers to opposing concepts or positions as opposites not reverse. For example, one would say the left is the opposite of the right, but not the reverse. Also, one typically refers to the antonym of a definition as the opposite, not the reverse.

Therefore, reverse is typically limited to physical motion, and more specifically, physical motion on the same line, plane or circle, but opposite can be used in regard to both physical and conceptual matters and is slightly more generic - but they cannot always be used interchangeably.

Also, its not always incorrect to refer to opposing concepts or positions as a reverse, Its just more common to refer to them as the opposite.

To go further into opposite:

Reverse and Opposite

The most common ways to think about opposite motion is:
- Extreme ends of anything - as in hand / foot, left / right, top / bottom, back / front
- Delivery / Retraction - as in moves
- Opposing directions - as in Close the Gap vs Open the Gap

To go further into reverse:

The most common ways to think about reverse motion is:
- Playing a video tape or movie backward.
- The same motion going in the opposite direction on the same line or plane

Appendix 4 - Categories and Category Completion

American Kenpo is a self-defense *system* - not just a martial art. What this means is that American Kenpo just isn't a way of studying the art of defending one's self against an opponent, but rather the study of human anatomy and movement as it relates to self-defense and martial ways. This distinction implies certain differences from other martial arts. For one, a system is a construct. A large part of American Kenpo is the complete (or as complete as can be obtained) analysis of human movement as it relates to combat. And, through this analysis principles, rules, theories, concepts, definitions, motions, and actions are derived and refined; with the end result being American Kenpo.

Category Completion is one of the most commonly used terms in American Kenpo. Many people use this term but never really understand what it means. The term Category Completion is almost self-defining - completing categories. But, what is a category, how do you determine a category, and how is it completed?

Categories and Catetory Completion

First - what is a category? By definition, a category is a grouping of something through a common property or aspect. In practice, a category is the attempt to determine all possible ways something can be accomplished, cataloging it, and ensuring that American Kenpo exposes this analysis somewhere in the system, some how.

Second - how do you determine a category? The best way to create a category is to define the boundaries of what you are analyzing and breaking it down into all possible permutations. The boundary can be extremely broad, extremely narrow, or anywhere in between. To get a better understanding of how to do this, browse through the examples in the following sections.

Third - How is this category completed? A category is completed by demonstrating the permutations of the category. In our case, via a form.

Finally, there is one subject that needs to be discussed - Purposeful Omission. Purposeful Omission is purposefully NOT demonstrating one of the permutations of a category. Usually this is done because a permutation of a category is determined to be non-useful and is therefore excluded from the completing of that category.

Category Completion - Example

The category has been determined as follows (boundaries): all downward blocks - executed as a block (not a parry) - with the hand closed. From these boundaries (category), one should deduce there are four (4) possible types of blocks:

- Inside-Downward, Palm Down
- Inside-Downward, Palm Up
- Outside-Downward, Palm Down
- Outside-Downward, Palm Up

In practice, one should further deduce that one of the blocks is non-useful - the Outside-Downward, Palm Up block. This is due to the limitations of human physical anatomy. This fourth block just can not be executed effectively. So, one should omit it from the demonstration of the category. This is exactly what is accomplished in the isolation of Long Form One. Of the three remaining downward blocks to be demonstrated, two are executed in the form - with the third being Purposefully Omitted.

Category Legend

The following sections are further examples of categories and how they are completed using both Short Form One and Long Form One as the basis of analysis. The Inter-Form Categories section analyzes categories that span multiple forms. The Intra-Form Categories section analyzes categories that are contained within Long Form One.

This is the legend for the following category tables:

Legend	
SF1	Short Form One
LF1	Long Form One
PO	Purposeful Omission
✓	Fulfilled
...	More to this Category

Inter-Form Categories

One thing to notice about these categories is that they start very broad and become more specific. This is generally how categories are created: A broad category is defined and then broken down into more specific categories. And, the cycle continues until no more categories can be created. Another thing to notice is that Long Form One completes some of the categories presented, but not all of them. This is an indication that there is more information somewhere else (in the higher forms) that will complete the category.

Category: Maneuver Type

	Defense	Offense
SF1	✓	
LF1	✓	✓

Category: Direction - Foot Maneuver

	Retreat	Advance
SF1	✓	
LF1	✓	✓

Category: Used Arm

	Left	Right
SF1	✓	✓
LF1	✓	✓

Category: Used Side

	Front	Rear
SF1	✓	
LF1	✓	✓

© 2014 EPAKS Publications

Categories and Catetory Completion | 363

Category: Hand Positioning

	Closed	Open
SF1	✓	
LF1	✓	✓

Category: Direction Blocked

	In	Out	Up	Down
SF1	✓	✓	✓	✓
LF1	✓	✓	✓	✓

Category: Direction Faced

	12:00	1:30	3:00	4:30	6:00	7:30	9:00	10:30
SF1	✓		✓		✓		✓	
LF1	✓		✓		✓		✓	

Category: Part of Body Used

	Arm	Hand	Elbow	Foot	Knee	...
SF1	✓					
LF1	✓	✓	✓			

Category: Part of Arm Used

	Forearm	Fist	Palm	Elbow	Fingers	Knuckle	...
SF1	✓						
LF1	✓	✓	✓	✓		✓	

© 2014 EPAKS Publications

Intra-Form Categories

Notice how most of these categories are started but not completed in Long Form One. This indicates that there is more information (in the higher forms) that will complete these categories.

Category: Part of Hand - Contact

	Knuckle	Finger	Palm	Hammer	Ridge	...
LF1	✓		✓			

Category: Type of Downward Block

	Inside Palm Up	Inside Palm Dn	Outside Palm Up	Outside Palm Dn
LF1	✓	✓	PO	✓

Category: Hand Positioning - Defense

	Closed	Open
LF1	✓	✓

Category: Hand Positioning - Offense

	Closed	Open
LF1	✓	

Category: Offense side

	Rear	Front
LF1	✓	✓

Category: Defense side

	Rear	Front
LF1	✓	✓

Index

- A -

Accumulative Journal 1.0	14
Accumulative Journal 2.0	16
Advanced	
Analysis	197
Analysis - Summary	205
Analysis - Walk Through	199
Quiz - Fill in the Blank	340
Quiz - Multiple Choice	333
Quiz Answers - Fill in the Blank	347
Quiz Answers - Multiple Choice	346
Summary - Analysis	205
Walk Through - Analysis	199
Analysis	176
Advanced	197
Advanced - Summary	205
Advanced - Walk Through	199
Beginning / Intermediate	181
Beginning / Intermediate - Summary	191
Beginning / Intermediate - Walk Through	183
Concepts	230
Definitions	230
Inter vs Intra Form	179
Opposite / Reverse	208
Principles	230
Reverse / Opposite	208
Rules	230
Summary - Advanced	205
Summary - Beginning / Intermediate	191

© 2014 EPAKS Publications

Analysis	176
Theories	230
Walk Through - Advanced	199
Walk Through - Beginning / Intermediate	183
Answers	
Quiz - Fill in the Blank - Advanced	347
Quiz - Fill in the Blank - Beginner / Intermediate	345
Quiz - Multiple Choice - Advanced	346
Quiz - Multiple Choice - Beginner / Intermediate	344
Appendix	
Category - Legend	361
Category Completion	358
Category Completion - Example	360
Category Completion - Inter-Form Categories	362
Category Completion - Intra-Form Categories	364
Opposite and Reverse	355
Reverse and Opposite	355

- B -

Basics	
Detailed Usage	169
Form	165
Quick Reference	167
Beginner / Intermediate	
Quiz - Fill in the Blank	330
Quiz - Multiple Choice	323
Quiz Answers - Fill in the Blank	345
Quiz Answers - Multiple Choice	344
Beginning / Intermediate	
Analysis	181
Analysis - Summary	191
Analysis - Walk Through	183

© 2014 EPAKS Publications

Beginning / Intermediate
    Summary - Analysis   191
    Walk Through - Analysis   183
Blocks
    Errors   269
    Errors - Overview   268
Blocks - Downward
    Errors   275
Blocks - Inside Downward (Palm Down)
    Errors   278
Blocks - Inside Downward (Palm Up)
    Errors   277
Blocks - Inward
    Errors   270
Blocks - Push Down
    Errors   279
Blocks - Upward
    Errors   273
Blocks - Vertical Outward
    Errors   271
Breathing
    Errors   239

- C -

Categories   358
Category   358
Category Completion   358
    Category - Legend   361
    Example   360
        Inter-Form Categories   362
        Intra-Form Categories   364

- D -

Design of Long Form One	159

- E -

Encyclopedia of Kenpo	16
Errors	
Blocks	269
Blocks - Downward	275
Blocks - Inside Downward (Palm Down)	278
Blocks - Inside Downward (Palm Up)	277
Blocks - Inward	270
Blocks - Overview	268
Blocks - Push Down	279
Blocks - Upward	273
Blocks - Vertical Outward	271
Breathing	239
Foot Maneuvers	262
Foot Maneuvers - Cover	266
Foot Maneuvers - Overview	260
Foot Maneuvers - Step Out (Meditating Horse)	263
Foot Maneuvers - Step Through	264
Gaze	238
Improvement Priorities	294
Overview	236
Stance	244
Stance - 45 Degree Cat	253
Stance - Fighting Horse	258
Stance - Forward Bow	250
Stance - Meditating Horse	245
Stance - Neutral Bow	247

© 2014 EPAKS Publications

Errors
- Stance - Overview — 241
- Stance - Reverse Bow — 255
- Strikes — 283
- Strikes - Angled Punches (Isolation) — 290
- Strikes - Outward Elbow — 288
- Strikes - Straight Punch — 284
- Strikes - Uppercut Punch (Isolation) — 292
- Strikes- Overview — 282
- Timing — 237

Execution — 65
- Blocking Errors — 269
- Blocking Errors - Downward — 275
- Blocking Errors - Inside Downward (Palm Down) — 278
- Blocking Errors - Inside Downward (Palm Up) — 277
- Blocking Errors - Inward — 270
- Blocking Errors - Overview — 268
- Blocking Errors - Push Down — 279
- Blocking Errors - Upward — 273
- Blocking Errors - Vertical Outward — 271
- Breathing Errors — 239
- Errors - Improvement Priorities — 294
- Foot Maneuver Errors — 262
- Foot Maneuver Errors - Cover — 266
- Foot Maneuver Errors - Overview — 260
- Foot Maneuver Errors - Step Out (Meditating Horse) — 263
- Foot Maneuver Errors - Step Through — 264
- Form Standard — 72
- Form Standard - Illustration — 90
- Form Standard - Video — 153
- Gaze Errors — 238
- General Errors - Overview — 236
- Improving — 234

© 2014 EPAKS Publications

Execution	65
Non-destructive Variations	68
Non-permanent Variations	67
Salutation, Standard	21
Salutation, Standard - Illustration	26
Stance Errors	244
Stance Errors - 45 Degree Cat	253
Stance Errors - Fighting Horse	258
Stance Errors - Forward Bow	250
Stance Errors - Meditating Horse	245
Stance Errors - Neutral Bow	247
Stance Errors - Overview	241
Stance Errors - Reverse Bow	255
Standard - Illustration	46
Striking Errors	283
Striking Errors - Angled Punches (Isolation)	290
Striking Errors - Outward Elbow	288
Striking Errors - Overview	282
Striking Errors - Straight Punch	284
Striking Errors - Uppercut Punch (Isolation)	292
Timing Errors	237
Variation Types	65
Various Standards	70

- F -

FAQ	296
Back foot settle with block or punch?	303
Cantact point of punch	310
Did SGM Parkger create this form?	320
Difference between opposite and reverse	314
Difference between Thrusting and Hammering	313
Straight punch primary Power Principle?	302
Timing of Form?	297

© 2014 EPAKS Publications

FAQ	296
Type of elbow	311
What is a dictionary form?	321
What is an isolation?	309
Where to look executing form	317
Why + pattern?	319
Why first move straight punch?	299
Why first punch left side?	301
Why no forward bow on triple blocks?	308
Why not defense only?	298
Why not lean?	318
Why not visualize opponent?	315
Why only one cat stance?	304
Why so much information in form?	316
Why step forward on first downward block?	307
Why triple blocks in second half?	306
Fill in the Blank	
Advanced - Quiz	340
Beginner / Intermediate - Quiz	330
Quiz Answers - Advanced	347
Quiz Answers - Beginner / Intermediate	345
Foot Maneuver	
Errors	262
Errors - Overview	260
Foot Maneuver - Cover	
Errors	266
Foot Maneuver - Step Out (Meditating Horse)	
Errors	263
Foot Maneuver - Step Through	
Errors	264

Gaze

- H -

Gaze	
Errors	238
History	11
During SGM Parker's Life	14
Inifinite Insight into Kenpo #5	14
Post SGM Parker Death	16

- I -

Illustration	
Fom Execution	90
Salutation, Standard Execution	26
Signifying, Standard Execution	46
Improvement Priorities	
Errors	294
Inter vs Intra Form Analysis	179
Introduction	9

- K -

Kenpo Kards	
Back of Kard	352
Front of Kard	350
Overview	348

- L -

Long Form One vs Short Form One	163

© 2014 EPAKS Publications

- M -

Multiple Choice	
Advanced - Quiz	333
Beginner / Intermediate - Quiz	323
Quiz Answers - Advanced	346
Quiz Answers - Beginner / Intermediate	344

- O -

Opposite	355
Opposite / Reverse	
Analysis	208
Opposite and Reverse	355

- Q -

Quiz	
Advanced - Fill in the Blank	340
Advanced - Multiple Choice	333
Answers - Fill in the Blank - Advanced	347
Answers - Fill in the Blank - Beginner / Intermediat	345
Answers - Multiple Choice - Advanced	346
Answers - Multiple Choice - Beginner / Intermediate	344
Answers - Overview	343
Beginner / Intermediate - Fill in the Blank	330
Beginner / Intermediate - Multiple Choice	323
Overview	322

- R -

Reverse	355
Reverse / Opposite	
Analysis	208
Reverse and Opposite	355

- S -

Salutation	19
Execution, Standard	21
Execution, Standard - Illustration	26
Standard Execution	21
Variations	43
Salutation and Signifying	18
Signifying	44
Execution, Standard - Illustration	46
Variations	63
Signing	44
Stance	
Errors	244
Errors - Overview	241
Stance - 45 Degree Cat	
Errors	253
Stance - Fighting Horse	
Errors	258
Stance - Forward Bow	
Errors	250
Stance - Meditating Horse	
Errors	245
Stance - Neutral Bow	
Errors	247
Stance - Reverse Bow	

| | Index | 375 |

Stance - Reverse Bow
    Errors   255
Standard
    Form Execution   72
    Form Execution - Illustration   90
    Form Execution - Video   153
    Salutation Execution   21
    Salutation Execution - Illustration   26
    Signifying Execution - Illustration   46
Strikes
    Errors   283
    Errors - Overview   282
Strikes - Angled Punches (Isolation)
    Errors   290
Strikes - Outward Elbow
    Errors   288
Strikes - Straight Punch
    Errors   284
Strikes - Uppercut Punch (Isolation)
    Errors   292
Summary
    Advanced - Analysis   205
    Analysis - Advanced   205
    Analysis - Beginning / Intermediate   191
    Beginning / Intermediate - Analysis   191

- T -

Timing
    Errors   237

- U -

Understanding

Understanding
    American Kenpo forms   154
    Long Form One   157
    Long Form One vs Short Form One   163
    The Design of Long Form One   159
    Why Long Form One   161

- V -

Video
    Form Execution   153

- W -

Walk-Through
    Advanced - Analysis   199
    Analysis - Advanced   199
    Analysis - Beginning / Intermediate   183
    Beginning / Intermediate - Analysis   183
Why Long Form One   161

© 2014 EPAKS Publications

www.ingramcontent.com/pod-product-compliance
Lightning Source LLC
Chambersburg PA
CBHW072002150426
43194CB00008B/965